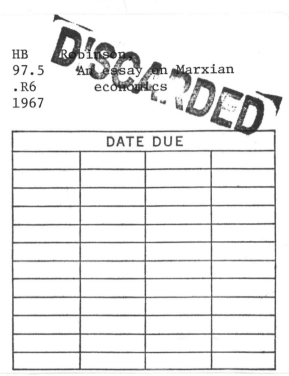

DATE DUE			

AN ESSAY ON
MARXIAN ECONOMICS

Books by Joan Robinson

AN ESSAY ON
MARXIAN ECONOMICS

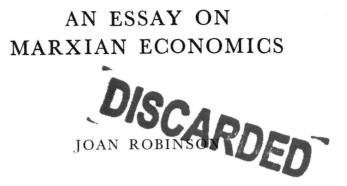

JOAN ROBINSON

Second Edition

First Edition (*Demy 8vo*) *1942*
Reissued (*Crown 8vo*) *1947*
Reprinted *1949, 1952, 1957, 1960, 1963, 1964*
Second Edition *1966*
Reprinted *1967, 1969, 1971, 1974, 1976*

Published by
THE MACMILLAN PRESS LTD
London and Basingstoke
Associated companies in New York Dublin
Melbourne Johannesburg and Madras

SBN (boards) 333 02081 2
(paperback) 333 05800 3

Printed in Great Britain by
LOWE AND BRYDONE PRINTERS LIMITED
Thetford, Norfolk

CONTENTS

PREFACE TO THE SECOND EDITION

In the twenty-five years since this book was written there has been much argument around the questions that it discusses, both on the academic and the Marxist side. In those days most of my academic colleagues in England thought that to study Marx was a quaint pastime (though Keynes, who was allergic to Marx's writing, received my *Essay* kindly) and in the United States it was disreputable. On the other side, any criticism of the master was thought impious, and the attempt to apply academic methods of analysis to his problems, futile.

Nowadays the academics are impatient of static analysis; the classical problems of growth and development have come back into fashion, reviving interest in the classical economists and Marx amongst them. The Marxists, on their side, are now ready to admit that some parts of the academic analysis can be separated from its unacceptable ideology and applied to real problems.

I began to read *Capital*, just as one reads any book, to see what was in it; I found a great deal that neither its followers nor its opponents had prepared me to expect. Piero Sraffa teased me, saying that I treated Marx as a little-known forerunner of Kalecki. There is a certain sense in which this is not a joke. There are many pointers in *Capital* to a theory of effective demand. Marx's disciples could have worked it out before Keynes and Kalecki learned it from the brutal teaching of the great slump; but they did not do so. The professed Marxists in England greeted the *General Theory* with the slogans of sound finance. The "Keynesian" element in Marx *was* little-known.

The academics did not even pretend to understand Marx. It seemed to me that, apart from prejudice, a barrier was created for them by his nineteenth-century metaphysical habits of thought, which are alien to a generation brought up to inquire into the meaning of meaning. I therefore tried to translate Marx's concepts into language that an academic could understand. This puzzled and angered the professed Marxists, to whom the metaphysic is precious for its own sake.

The task of translation is now much easier than it was at that time.

I

Exploitation. For Marx himself the theory of exploitation, that is, the theory of the distribution of the net product of industry between wages and profits, emerged from the theory of *value*, in the sense of a theory of the relative prices of commodities. The association between the two has been a plentiful source of confusion.

To separate them, consider an economy consisting of capitalists and workers (land is free) whose only product is Ricardo's "corn". There are no prices of commodities, since there is only one commodity. The only price in the system is the corn price of labour time — the real-wage rate. The technical conditions of production determine the net product per man-year of work — that is, the harvest minus seed corn divided by the number of men employed. The corn-wage rate then determines the profit per man employed. The ratio of profit, or surplus, to the wage is the rate of exploitation. The rate of profit on capital is determined at the same time. An employer who is keeping his capital intact divides the harvest into two parts. One is a stock to provide seed corn and wages for next year, replacing the stock that has been used up over the past year, and the other is the income that he can consume, including in consumption payments to servants, priests, harlots, etc. — the unproductive workers. The ratio of this income to the stock is the rate of profit.

Now, it seems obvious that this analysis cannot be affected, in essence, by allowing for a variety of commodities. The commodities may be supposed to be sold at prices which yield a uniform rate of profit on all capital. This introduces some troublesome problems of measuring net output and the stock of capital, since relative prices will change with the real-wage rate, but it does not alter the main line of the argument.

All the pother about *value* and prices permitted the academics to evade the penetrating analysis of exploitation that Marx had derived from Ricardo. At the same time it concealed from the Marxists the fact that they had not been provided with an explicit theory of distribution of their own.

Marx abandoned the subsistence minimum in terms of corn which is the linchpin of Ricardo's system and allowed for a vague historical determination of real wages. When capitalists first invade the artisan and peasant economy, they must pay a wage which permits more or less the customary standard of life to be maintained. Thereafter, in Volume I of *Capital*, the existence of the reserve army of labour keeps the level of wages more or less constant, though there may be phases of rising wages when the accumulation of capital runs ahead of the growth of the available labour force. But in Volume III, in connection with the falling rate of profits, we encounter a constant rate of exploitation, along with rising productivity. In Volume I, labour-saving technical progress tends to raise the rate of exploitation and is likely to lower the wage rate, because it reduces the demand for labour. In Volume III it leaves the rate of exploitation more or less constant, and the rate of profit on capital is squeezed. The movements of the level of wages in Volume I depend upon the relative bargaining strength of capitalists and workers and on the political balance of power. The constant rate of exploitation in Volume III is not explained, and the fact that it entails a rising level of real wages is not noticed. I was much startled when I came upon this in reading *Capital* for the first time. None of the discussions and controversies I have had since have cleared the point up.

Both situations are met with in real life. In modern industrialised countries the rate of exploitation is fairly steady and the real-wage level is normally rising as technical progress raises productivity, while the picture drawn in Volume I broadly corresponds to the situation of many underdeveloped economies. It is a great merit of Marx's method that it lends itself to historical interpretation, unlike the mechanical equilibrium theory of the academics, but the attempts of the fundamentalists of Marxism to believe in the growing misery of the workers and the falling rate of profit at the same time have caused a lot of confusion.

Relative Prices. The *value* of the flow of output of a particular commodity is the net product of the current labour required to manufacture it (corresponding to the wage bill together with the surplus), plus the *value* of the raw materials used up in the process and replacement of the *value* of the depreciation of the equipment involved, all expressed as a quantity of labour time. Marx opens his analysis of capitalism by declaring that commodities normally exchange at prices proportional to their *values*.

For him this was the vital clue to the whole problem.

If prices were proportional to *values*, net proceeds from sales of the output of a man-hour of labour time would be uniform for all commodities, so that, with a uniform wage rate, there would be a uniform ratio of profits to wages. Marx was not ignorant of Ricardo's difficulty — that for technical reasons different commodities require different ratios of capital to labour, and competition between capitalists tends to establish prices that yield a uniform rate of profit on capital so that a uniform ratio of profits to wages cannot obtain — but he evidently felt that *in some sense* the law of *value* is true all the same.

This ancient puzzle has now been cleared up by the publication of Sraffa's *Production of Commodities by Means of Commodities*; the famous problem of the transformation of values into prices has been laid to rest. In given technical conditions there is a pattern of prices corresponding to each rate of profit. Prices are proportionate to *values* when the rate of profit is zero. (Keynes, by the way, pointed this out to me when he read my little book.)

With positive rates of profit, prices would be proportionate to values only if all commodities required the same ratio of capital to labour. It is sometimes maintained that, in Volume I, Marx was intending this situation to be assumed. If so, Ricardo's difficulty was simply ruled out. This would seem to support my contention that, once the overall rate of exploitation is given, relative prices are not particularly interesting.

As a historical process the prices of manufactures were evolved as capitalism gradually conquered the peasant and artisan economy. At first the level of wages that it was necessary to pay was set by the level of earnings of artisans, while the prices of commodities were limited by the prices of handicraft products. The higher level of output per head of workers organised in capitalist enterprises determined the share of profit in the selling value of output. Professor Bensusan Butt[1] provides a model in which capitalism first attacks the product where its superiority over handicraft production is greatest, and absorbs it all before attacking the next, so that, at any moment, there is a uniform rate of profit within the capitalist sector, falling as time goes by. Historically, however, capitalism attacked at several points at once. Each commodity at first must have had its own rate of exploitation and its own rate of profit. Competition then set to work to equalise the rate of profit. There is no reason to postulate any tendency for the rates of exploitation to be equalised, so as to make prices proportionate to *values*.

As a logical process, the ratio of profits to wages for each individual commodity, can be calculated when the rate of profit is known. The transformation is from prices into *values*, not the other way.

Therefore, in spite of the offence which it has given, I cannot withdraw the remark at the end of Chapter III. The concept of *value* seems to me to be a remarkable example of how a metaphysical notion can inspire original thought, though in itself it is quite devoid of operational meaning.

Constant and variable capital. In the stationary corn economy described above, the wage bill, that is, the corn paid out to the workers over a year, is identically the same thing as the wage fund, that is, a part of the revolving stock of corn that reappears after each harvest sufficient to replace the wages paid out last year. Marx explicitly takes a period of production such that the wage bill and the wage fund are equal, and uses one symbol, v, for

[1] *On Economic Growth* (Oxford, 1960).

both. The wage fund he calls *variable capital*, because it is the part of capital used to purchase current labour time, which creates *value*, as opposed to raw materials and equipment, which pass on to current output only the constant amount of *value* embodied in them at the time when they were produced.

The distinction between variable and constant capital, which had great significance for Marx, belongs to the metaphysical level of his thought. Moreover, there seems to be some confusion on the analytical level. It is in its aspect as the wage bill that the corn allows the capitalist to employ living labour and to extract a surplus from production. The wage fund is important only because it permits him to pay out the wage bill. The capitalist can extract the surplus because output per head, when labour is organised by him, exceeds the wage by more than is required to replace seed corn. When he provides machinery, output per head will be higher and the surplus that he can extract is thereby increased. The whole of his capital, not merely the wage fund, is engaged in the process of exploitation.

We can improve the analytical apparatus by providing more symbols. Let us write (in terms of any appropriate unit) v for the wage bill, V for the wage fund; c for the raw materials and depreciation of equipment, and C for the stock of capital in existence, excluding the wage fund. Thus, $C + V$ is the stock of capital, and $c + v + s$ is gross product per annum. Then $v + s$ is net output; s/v is the rate of exploitation: $s/(C + V)$ is the rate of profit. There does not seem to be any way of writing the third ratio — the organic composition of capital — that makes sense, for neither c/v nor C/V corresponds to the idea which it expresses. It is clear enough, however, that what Marx has in mind, when he is talking about organic composition, is the relation of past labour time embodied in the stock of capital goods to labour time currently employed. This relationship has a physical aspect, as a description of the technique of production, and a financial aspect — the value of capital, in terms of purchasing power over commodities, per man employed.

Marx's generalisation that, as a historical process, the organic composition of capital tends to rise as capitalism develops means that capital in terms of labour time per unit of current labour employed tends to rise. This corresponds to saying that technical progress has a capital-using bias, so that, when the rate of profit is constant, the share of profit in value of output tends to rise.

By the same token, when the share of profit is constant (the rate of exploitation is constant), the rate of profit tends to fall.

Whether there is a predominant tendency for accumulation to have a capital-using bias, and, when it has, whether the share of profit or the rate of profit is more nearly constant, are questions of historical fact, not of logical necessity. So far as the evidence goes, it does not seem to suggest that in developed industrial economies there is any clear and continuous bias of accumulation to the capital-using side. When capitalism invades a peasant economy, certainly, it introduces capital-using techniques. But then, by the very same process, it is reducing employment and raising output per head, so that the rate of exploitation is raised and there is no reason to expect the rate of profit on capital to be falling — rather the reverse.

2

These points are concerned with Marx's analytical apparatus. We can now turn to wider themes.

Employment and Wages. It is generally recognised nowadays that unemployment due to a failure of effective demand (often called "Keynesian") must be distinguished from the non-employment (often called "Marxian") which comes about when the available supply of labour is growing faster than the number of jobs offered by the capitalist economy. Marx thinks of the supply of labour as being fed by the ruin of the peasant and artisan economy. In his anxiety to combat the reactionary views of Malthus he refused to admit that a rapid growth of population is deleterious to the interests of the working class. This seems to be an aberration, inconsistent with the main line of his theory.

It is also now recognised that a frontal attack upon money-wage rates, in a developed industrial economy, cannot effectively reduce the rate of exploitation (the share of profits in net value of output), because profit margins will generally be maintained simply by raising money prices proportionately. On the other hand, to call off the struggle and keep money-wage rates constant, would be likely to allow the rate of exploitation to rise, for money prices would be held more or less constant while costs gradually fell as a result of technical progress. (Imperfect competition cannot be relied upon to limit margins — rather it fills up the gap with selling costs and advertisement of all kinds.) This kind of rise in profits is not healthy for the capitalists, as it is associated with a restriction upon the purchasing power of the workers, so that effective demand fails to expand with productive capacity. Thus the struggles of the trade unions, though they do not succeed in reducing the relative share of profits, save the capitalists from the ill effects of increasing it.

On these points further discussion and experience

seems to have confirmed the views that I was trying to express in my *Essay*, but it seems to me now that I applied them in a very parochial manner. Marx was describing capitalism in the period of its expansion. When I was writing it had already passed its peak, and since then its area of operation has sharply contracted. Socialism has come into existence, not as Marx predicted, from the internal disintegration of overripe capitalism, but outside it.

Schumpeter, in *Capitalism, Socialism and Democracy* (published just after my *Essay*), remarked: "It must be remembered that the bolshevik conquest of rule over the most backward of all the great nations was nothing but a fluke." I commented at the time: "Perhaps. But in that case the exception seems rather more important than the rule. Who knows what flukes may accompany the end of the present war?" There is certainly some element of geographical accident in the selection of countries and parts of countries in which socialist régimes have been set up, but there is clearly an underlying pattern. It is not a fluke that they are among the formerly most backward from the point of view of industrial development.

Meanwhile capitalism seems to be enjoying a second lease of life; exploitation can no longer be represented as a cause of increasing misery. Rather it offers a privileged position in the world that makes the industrial working class a conservative rather than a revolutionary force. Misery is increasing, certainly, but it is increasing outside the orbit of both socialism and capitalism, where the available labour force grows faster than exploitation can keep up with it.

The world picture has slipped out of the frame of Marx's argument. But the questions that he posed are still relevant today, while the academics continue to erect elegant elaborations on trivial topics.

3

The Rate of Profit and the Rate of Exploitation. The account which I gave of the orthodox theory of profits, or rather of the lack of a theory, in the setting of the stationary state, was challenged by Gerald Shove.[1] He maintained that Marshall intended by "normal profits" the rate of profit compatible with a steady, foreseen rate of growth. Abnormal profits then result from unexpected changes in the growth of demand for particular commodities. This reading of Marshall is certainly as plausible as the static interpretation. The trouble with Marshall is that he expects us to believe both at once; and in neither does he give a coherent account of what determines the "normal" rate of profit. Wicksell was sufficiently candid to admit that he had not found a satisfactory theory. Contemporary neo-neoclassics (the dominant school in the United States) have broken out of the stationary state and regard accumulation as normal, but they have got themselves stuck in the same bog as the old neoclassics by trying to define a quantity of capital independently of the rate of profit. This may appear to be merely a subject for logic-chopping, but it has its roots in the old metaphysical question of whether "capital", as well as labour, produces *value*.

The Keynesian branch of the academic school has developed a theory of the rate of profit which has a close affinity with Marx's scheme of expanded reproduction. When all saving comes out of profit, expenditure by workers covers the wage bill. Net profits for any period are then equal to net investment plus consumption out of profits. The ratio of net investment to the value of capital is the rate of accumulation. It follows that the rate of

[1] "Mrs. Robinson on Marxian Economics", *Economic Journal* (April 1944), p. 60.

profit is equal to the rate of accumulation divided by the ratio of saving to profit.[1] The rate of accumulation is determined (as in Marx's view) by the energy of the capitalists. When the labour force is not growing fast enough to accommodate the accumulation that they want to carry out it is supplemented by technical progress. Thus it is possible, though by no means necessary, for capitalism to enjoy long runs of continuous growth with a constant rate of profit.

This provides a theory of the rate of profit, which was lacking before; but the argument is still superficial. If some deeper-lying economic relationships determine the rate of exploitation, capitalists' accumulation and consumption are limited by it. The *rate* of profit is then, as Marx maintained, the result of the manner in which competition shares out the *mass* of profit that the system generates.

The famous mystery of the constant relative shares of wages and profits in the product of industry does not now seem particularly mysterious. Trade Unions, backed by social legislation, oppose a countervailing power to monopoly that keeps the balance of forces fairly even. Neither party can succeed in increasing its relative share appreciably, while more-or-less neutral technical progress makes a more-or-less constant rate of exploitation compatible with a more-or-less constant rate of profit over the long run.

But the notion that relative shares are uniform over the world, which seems to have been current when I was writing my *Essay*, is simply false. A very interesting inquiry published by the United Nations Department for

[1] P = profit per annum, I = net investment per annum, K = value of capital, s = proportion of profits saved. $I = sP, \quad \dfrac{P}{K} = \dfrac{I}{K} \cdot \dfrac{I}{s}.$

Economic and Social Affairs,[1] which has been very little publicised in academic quarters, shows the share of wages in value of net output of manufacturing industry varying from less than 25 per cent in countries such as Nicaragua and Costa Rica to more than 50 per cent in Australia, the Scandinavian countries, the United Kingdom and the United States, while in countries such as Italy and Japan it is around 40 per cent. These figures certainly suggest that the clue to relative shares is to be found in bargaining power, rather than in the capital/labour ratio.

4

Value under Socialism. There is a third element in the complex notion of *value* besides the theory of exploitation and the theory of relative prices, that is, the ideal of the *just price* — the concept that it is right and rational for the worker to receive the *value* that he produces. Under capitalism this is not possible, since the capitalists must squeeze the surplus out of him to accumulate, but under socialism the law of *value* will come into its own, for Marx expected socialism to be installed after capitalism had fulfilled its historic task of accumulation. He assumed that some investment would still be made under socialism, but it did not seem to him particularly important. Socialism, in fact, has come into existence in under-developed economies, surrounded by enemies. Instead of being able to distribute the surplus to the workers, it has been obliged to squeeze out all the more, for industrialisation and for defence.

The Soviet economists feel obliged to argue in terms of *value* but they do not make it comprehensible. In all the socialist countries the greater part of agriculture is in the hands of peasants, or of co-operatives, of one kind and

[1] *Patterns of Industrial Growth*, 1938–58 (1960).

another, which share with a peasant economy the characteristic that the income of a group of workers depends upon the produce of the particular area of land that has been allotted to them. The equivalent of the money-wage rate for an agricultural worker, that is, the money return for a labour-day in a co-operative, depends upon the price of the products of that particular farm. There is no way in which prices can be derived from *values*.

The principle of justice suggests that prices for agricultural products, in relation to money-wage rates in industry, ought to be such as to equalise real incomes between the two sectors. In practice justice has been overborne by political necessity. Even if it could be accepted in principle, it is not easy to see what it would mean. The style of life of the two groups of households is necessarily different, and so is the kind of effort required of them. How could "equal pay for equal work" be assessed? When an economy is sufficiently developed to offer a choice of career to individuals, it becomes necessary to make country life sufficiently attractive to keep an adequate agricultural labour force in being. The principle of justice then reduces to the principle of supply price.

There is another difficulty. Because of differences in fertility, climate, convenience to markets, etc., income is easier to earn in some areas than others. Justice and efficiency both require differential rent to be extracted from the farmers and paid to the national economy. This is beginning to be recognised in principle, but it is not easy to carry it out in practice.

In the socialist sector of the economy, the level of money-wage rates and the technique of production determine costs in terms of money. The overall level of prices of goods sold to the public must yield an overall surplus sufficient to provide for the incomes of workers engaged in investment, free social services, defence, administration, etc. The debate about the law of *value* is concerned with how this surplus should be allocated between commodities. (Whether it is collected by means of taxes or of planned profits is a matter of administrative convenience rather than economic principle.) If every enterprise, at all stages of production, paid a uniform tax proportional to its wage bill, and prices at each stage were equal to costs including the tax, then final prices would be proportionate to *values*, but no such system has been found acceptable. Some would-be reformers amongst socialist economists advocate a system of Marx's prices of production — that is a system in which the surplus is collected in the form of a uniform rate of profit on capital invested. This is not in accordance with academic doctrine; in the theory of competition, prospective profits govern investment decisions, but once an investment has been made, bygones are bygones, and marginal, not average, cost comes into play. Nor does it seem to recommend itself to natural justice; why should the costs of defence, for instance, be levied from the consumers of different commodities in proportion to capital invested?

In any case, the philosophical discussion is quite beside the point, because no system of prices based upon costs will prove practicable. In any actual situation there is limited productive capacity for particular commodities; when goods are distributed through the market mechanism, not by rationing or queueing, the pattern of prices must be such as to induce the public to buy the goods that are available. The dominating principle must be to get a fit between demand and supply. The socialist economies have learned this the hard way.

Prices have the function not only of distributing goods

to consumers, but also of acting as an indicator of the efficiency of producers. In every line, there are low- and high-cost producers, through no merit or fault of their own — some factories are better equipped, some mines easier to work, and so forth. To stimulate efficiency, planned profits should not be too easy for the low-cost enterprises to achieve, nor hopeless for the high-cost enterprises. Costs should be reckoned on the basis of an efficient high-cost enterprise, and a rent charged to the low-cost enterprises, assessed on the basis of their differential advantages.

Here the academics can score a point against Marx, who always reckoned in terms of average cost, because in this connection the principle of marginal cost, or rather cost at the margin, corresponds to common sense.

My note on this subject (the Appendix to Chapter III, p. 23) now appears very old-fashioned, for much experience has since accumulated about price policy under socialism.

At the present time several socialist countries in Europe, finding the system evolved in the course of rapid accumulation inappropriate to the stage of potential affluence that they have now reached, are trying to introduce some features of a market economy into their planning. Meanwhile, the capitalist economies, finding that free enterprise cannot be relied upon to produce satisfactory results, are trying to introduce some features of planning into their market economies.

On both sides, a radical rethinking of the theory of prices is evidently required.

1965   JOAN ROBINSON

FOREWORD

THE purpose of this essay is to compare the economic analysis of Marx's *Capital* with current academic teaching. The comparison is, in one sense, a violent anachronism, for the development of Marx's thought was influenced by controversy with his own contemporaries, not with mine. But if we are interested, not in the historical evolution of economic theory, but in its possible future progress, this is the relevant comparison to make.

Until recently, Marx used to be treated in academic circles with contemptuous silence, broken only by an occasional mocking footnote. But modern developments in academic theory, forced by modern developments in economic life — the analysis of monopoly and the analysis of unemployment — have shattered the structure of orthodox doctrine and destroyed the complacency with which economists were wont to view the working of *laisser-faire* capitalism. Their attitude to Marx, as the leading critic of capitalism, is therefore much less cocksure than it used to be. In my belief, they have much to learn from him. The chief difficulty in learning from him arises from the peculiar language and the crabbed method of argument which he used, and my purpose is to explain what I understand Marx to have been saying in language intelligible to the academic economist.

At the same time, I believe that modern academic economics has something to offer to the Marxists. First, a reconsideration of Marx's argument in the light of the more precise and refined methods of modern analysis clears up many obscurities in his theory, and helps to reveal its strong and weak points. Second, in the analysis of effective demand — the theory of employment — modern economics provides a basis for the study of the law of motion of capitalism, which is suggested, but not fully developed, by Marx himself. Moreover, both parties must gain from attempting to understand their mutual criticisms, instead of indulging in ill-informed abuse.

I have confined my argument to Marx's economic analysis in the narrow sense, and made no attempt to deal with the broad treatment of history and sociology which forms the most important part of Marx's doctrine. This specialised approach is perhaps an unnatural one, and it is true that no particular aspect of Marx's argument can be properly understood without a grasp of the whole. But at the same time a detailed study of particular aspects is also useful, and the aspect which I have chosen to discuss is one of the highest importance in the development of the whole.

The first volume of *Das Kapital* was published by Marx in 1867. After his death in 1883 Engels edited the manuscripts for the remaining two volumes, which consisted partly of finished sections, and partly of uncompleted or overlapping rough drafts. Volume II was published in 1885 and Volume III in 1894.

There is a good deal of repetition in *Capital*, and where I have referred to a particular passage I have generally chosen somewhat arbitrarily between a number which make the same point. The references are intended as a gage of good faith rather than as a guide to reading *Capital*. References are to *Capital*, Volume I, published by Glaisher, 1920; Volume II, published by Swan Sonnenschein, 1907; and Volume III, published by Kerr, 1909. The references are numbered, and the title of the chapter and section in which each passage referred to occurs is given on pp. 96-101 for the convenience of readers using other editions.

I am much indebted to Mr. E. Rothbarth for many helpful discussions and criticisms.

JOAN ROBINSON

CAMBRIDGE
September 1941

NOTE

I HAVE made a small number of alterations in the text of the first edition of this book. The only one of substance is in the appendix to Chapter III where there was an error in my original argument.

JOAN ROBINSON

CAMBRIDGE
November 1946

CHAPTER I

INTRODUCTION

THE fundamental differences between Marxian and traditional orthodox economics are, first, that the orthodox economists accept the capitalist system as part of the eternal order of Nature, while Marx regards it as a passing phase in the transition from the feudal economy of the past to the socialist economy of the future. And, second, that the orthodox economists argue in terms of a harmony of interests between the various sections of the community, while Marx conceives of economic life in terms of a conflict of interests between owners of property who do no work and workers who own no property. These two points of difference are not unconnected — for if the system is taken for granted and the shares of the various classes in the social product are determined by inexorable natural law, all interests unite in requiring an increase in the total to be divided. But if the possibility of changing the system is once admitted, those who hope to gain and those who fear to lose by the change are immediately ranged in opposite camps.

The orthodox economists, on the whole, identified themselves with the system and assumed the role of its apologists, while Marx set himself to understand the working of capitalism in order to hasten its overthrow. Marx was conscious of his purpose. The economists were in general unconscious. They wrote as they did because it seemed to them the only possible way to write, and they believed themselves to be endowed with scientific impartiality. Their preconceptions emerge rather in the problems which they chose to study and the assumptions on which they worked than in overt political doctrine.

Since they believed themselves to be in search of eternal principles they paid little attention to the special historical features of actual situations, and, in particular, they were apt to project the economics of a community of small equal proprietors into the analysis of advanced capitalism. Thus the orthodox conception of competition entails that each commodity in each market is supplied by a large number of producers, acting individualistically, bound together neither by open collusion nor by unconscious class loyalty; and entails that any individual is free to enter any line of activity he pleases. And the laws derived from such a society are applied to modern industry and finance.

Again, the orthodox conception of wages tending to equal the *marginal disutility* of labour, which has its origin in the picture of a peasant farmer leaning on his hoe in the evening and deciding whether the extra product of another hour's work will repay the extra backache, is projected into the modern labour market, where the individual worker has no opportunity to decide anything except whether it is better to work or to starve.

The orthodox economists have been much preoccupied with elegant elaborations of minor problems, which distract the attention of their pupils from the uncongenial realities of the modern world, and the development of abstract argument has run far ahead of any possibility of empirical verification. Marx's intellectual tools are far cruder, but his sense of reality is far stronger, and his argument towers above their intricate constructions in rough and gloomy grandeur.

He sees the capitalist system as fulfilling a historic

mission to draw out the productive power of combined and specialised labour. From its birthplace in Europe it stretches out tentacles over the world to find its nourishment. It forces the accumulation of capital, and develops productive technique, and by these means raises the wealth of mankind to heights undreamed of in the peasant, feudal or slave economies.

But the workers, who, under the compulsion of capitalism, produce the wealth, obtain no benefit from the increase in their productive power. All the benefit accrues to the class of capitalists, for the efficiency of large-scale enterprise breaks down the competition of the peasant and the craftsman, and reduces all who have not property enough to join the ranks of the capitalists to selling their labour for the mere means of existence. Any concession which the capitalist makes to the worker is the concession which the farmer makes to his beasts — to feed them better that they may work the more.

The struggle for life binds the workers together and sets them in opposition to the propertied class, while the concentration of capital in ever larger concerns, forced on by the development of technique, turns the capitalists towards the anti-social practices of monopoly.

But the condemnation of the system does not only depend upon its moral repugnance, and the inevitability of its final overthrow does not only depend upon the determination of the workers to secure their rightful share in the product of their labour. The system contains contradictions within itself which must lead to its disruption. Marx sees the periodic crises of the trade cycle as symptoms of a deep-seated and progressive malady in the vitals of the system.

Developments in economic analysis which have taken place since Marx's day enable us to detect three distinct strands of thought in Marx's treatment of crises. There is, first, the theory of the reserve army of unemployed labour, which shows how unemployment tends to fluctuate with the relationship between the stock of capital offering employment to labour and the supply of labour available to be employed. Second, there is the theory of the falling rate of profit, which shows how the capitalists' greed for accumulation stultifies itself by reducing the average rate of return on capital. And thirdly, there is the theory of the relationship of capital-good to consumption-good industries, which shows the ever-growing productive power of society knocking against the limitation upon the power to consume which is set by the poverty of the workers.

In Marx's mind these three theories are not distinct, and are fused together in a single picture of the system, racked by its own inherent contradictions, generating the conditions for its own disintegration.

Meanwhile, the academic economists, without paying much attention to Marx, have been forced by the experiences of modern times to question much of the orthodox apologetic, and recent developments in academic theory have led them to a position which in some respects resembles the position of Marx far more closely than the position of their own intellectual forebears. The modern theory of imperfect competition, though formally quite different from Marx's theory of exploitation, has a close affinity with it. The modern theory of crises has many points of contact with the third line of argument, distinguished above, in Marx's treatment of the subject, and allows room for something resembling the first. Only the second line of argument — the falling rate of profit — appears confused and redundant.

In general, the nightmare quality of Marx's thought gives it, in this bedevilled age, an air of greater reality than the gentle complacency of the orthodox academics. Yet he, at the same time, is more encouraging than they, for he releases hope as well as terror from Pandora's box, while they preach only the gloomy doctrine that all is for the best in the best of all *possible* worlds.

But though Marx is more sympathetic, in many ways, to a modern mind, than the orthodox economists, there is no need to turn him, as many seek to do, into an inspired prophet. He regarded himself as a serious thinker, and it is as a serious thinker that I have endeavoured to treat him in the following pages.

The next five chapters contain an outline of Marx's argument, looked at from the point of view of a modern academic economist. Chapter VII contrasts his theory with the orthodox doctrine. Chapters VIII and IX, on the theory of employment and imperfect competition, show the movement of modern academic teaching away from orthodoxy in the direction of Marx. Chapter X, on wages, discusses a problem in which the movement has been in the opposite direction, so that Marx for once appears, from the modern point of view, to be in the orthodox camp. Chapter XI briefly enumerates the unsolved problems which all three parties leave open.

CHAPTER II

DEFINITIONS

MARX divides the net product of industry into two parts: *variable capital* and *surplus*. Variable capital (v) is the wages bill.[1] Surplus (s), which covers net profit, interest and rent,[2] is the excess of net product over wages. The difference between gross and net product is *constant capital* (c), which consists of plant and raw materials. It is *constant* in the sense that it adds no more to the value of output than it loses in the process of production, new value added being due to the labour-power purchased by variable capital.[3] Fixed plant contributes to c only in respect to its rate of wear and tear and depreciation.[4] Thus c consists of depreciation *plus* raw materials. The total product for any period, say a year, is then represented by $c + v + s$. These quantities are measured in *value*, or *socially necessary labour-time*.[5] This concept involves some problems which will be discussed in the next chapter.

Marx conducts his argument in terms of three ratios: $\frac{s}{v}$, the *rate of exploitation*,[6] $\frac{c}{v}$, the *organic composition of capital*,[7] and $\frac{s}{c + v}$, the *rate of profit*.[8]

The rate of exploitation, $\frac{s}{v}$, is the ratio of surplus (net profit, interest and rent) to wages, and indicates the share of labour in net output. Marx often expresses it as a

---

[1] Vol. I, p. 192[(1)].   [2] Vol. I, p. 194[(2)] and Vol. III, p. 993[(3)].
[3] Vol. I, p. 191[(4)]. See also below, p. 13.   [4] Vol. I, p. 195[(5)].
[5] Vol. I, p. 5[(6)].   [6] Vol. I, p. 198[(7)].
[7] Vol. I, p. 625[(8)].   [8] Vol. III, p. 55[(9)].

division of the working day into the time which a man works for himself and the time which he works for the capitalist. Thus if $\frac{s}{v}$ equals $\frac{3}{2}$, and the working day is 10 hours, a man works 4 hours for himself and 6 hours for his employer. He does 4 hours of "necessary" or "paid" labour, and 6 hours of "surplus" or "unpaid" labour.[1] This ratio plays the leading part in Marx's whole argument.

The rate of exploitation is unambiguous. The other two ratios, $\frac{c}{v}$ and $\frac{s}{c+v}$, involve some confusion. Both the organic composition of capital and the rate of profit are connected with the stock of capital employed, not with the depreciation of capital. To turn $c+v$ into the stock of capital we must refine upon Marx's categories and break up c into depreciation and raw materials, say d and r. Then $r+v$ and d must each be multiplied by the appropriate period of turnover. Suppose, for instance, that working capital represents on average six-months outlay on wages and raw materials, and that the average life of plant is ten years. Then $r+v$ must be divided by 2, and d multiplied by 10, in order to reduce $c+v$ to the stock of capital. Marx was aware of these points,[2] but his terminology obscures them. We can avoid ambiguity, without falsifying Marx's meaning, if we use the symbols c, v and s only for rates per unit of time of depreciation and raw material cost, wages and profit, and speak of the organic composition of capital, not as $\frac{c}{v}$, but as capital per man employed.

[1] Vol. I, p. 199[10].
[2] Vol. II, p. 190[11], and Vol. III, chap. 4[12]. This chapter was supplied by Engels, a sign, perhaps, that Marx found the subject perplexing or tedious.

The conception of capital per man employed raises a further difficulty. It can vary in three different ways. Slump conditions increase capital per man simply by reducing the level of employment while equipment remains unchanged; [1] the process of accumulation tends to increase capital per man at a given level of utilisation; finally, technical progress and changes in the rate of interest and of real wages may alter capital per man (given utilisation) in either direction. Marx assumes that capital is always used to capacity.[2] Moreover, he assumes that the capacity output of a given amount of capital is rigidly determined by technical conditions. The rate of interest has no influence on the capital structure, and the rate of real wages affects it only indirectly, through its influence on technical progress.[3]

These assumptions are fundamental to his whole argument. They rule out two sets of problems which, since Marx's day, have received much attention from academic economists: problems connected with the proportions of the factors of production employed in equilibrium, and problems connected with changes in the utilisation of capital equipment in response to changes in the state of trade. These points will be discussed later. The assumptions make a drastic simplification of a very complex problem, and, from an academic point of view, appear somewhat crude. But Marx avoids using certain no less

[1] Since Marx does not discuss this question explicitly, it is doubtful how he regarded it. He might be interpreted as regarding a decline in utilisation as equivalent to a reduction in capital. But this method of reckoning is excessively awkward, for it means that the rate of change of the stock of capital is not the same thing as the rate of accumulation.

[2] This assumption is not stated explicitly, but it is taken for granted that, in a given state of technique, there is only one amount of labour that a given amount of capital will employ, *e.g.* Vol. III, p. 291[13].

[3] Vol. I, p. 653[14].

drastic simplifications which the academic economists have become accustomed to employ, and he conducts his argument in dynamic terms, while they are for the most part confined to a more exact but less interesting analysis of static conditions.

CHAPTER III

THE LABOUR THEORY OF VALUE

MARX's theory of value has caused much confusion and generated much controversy. It seems, certainly, perplexing as we follow the uphill struggle of Marx's own mind from the simple dogmatism of the first volume of *Capital* to the intricate formulations of Volume III. But if we start from the vantage ground of Volume III the journey is much less arduous.

Capital is accumulating, the capitalist system is conquering fresh spheres from peasant and handicraft economies, the population is increasing and technical inventions are being made. Real wages, in general, remain constant at the level established in the pre-capitalist peasant economy,[1] or, rather, fluctuate around that level as capitalists' demand for labour varies relatively to the available supply.[2] The total surplus, in real terms, is the ever-increasing difference between total output and total real wages. The organic composition of capital, dictated by technical conditions, is different in different spheres.[3] The rate of profit on capital tends towards equality in all spheres, for the flow of new capital is attracted towards more than average profits and repelled by less than average profits.[4] Temporary differences in the rate of profit in particular industries may be due to demand (which in turn is determined by the distribution of income between workers and capitalists).[5] These are evened out

[1] See below, p. 30, n. 3.   [2] See below, p. 32.   [3] Vol. III, p. 172[15].
    [4] Vol. III, p. 230[16] and p. 243[17].   [5] Vol. III, p. 214[18].

by a relative increase in capital, and therefore in output, where demand is relatively high.[1]   Or they may be due to new techniques, which lower costs of production.   These are evened out by the action of competition, which gradually forces the general adoption of the new methods, and lowers the price of the commodity concerned.[2]   Since profit per unit of capital tends to be equal, and capital per man employed is not equal, the rate of exploitation (profit per man) is not equal, in different industries.   It tends to be above the average where capital per man is above the average.[3]

Where available land is limited, and varies in respect to fertility and site-value, private property in land enables its owners to exact a rent from the capitalists.[4]   Rent is paid out of the surplus obtained by capital, but since profit per unit of capital tends to equality in all lines of activity, the rate of exploitation must be higher the greater the rent that is paid.   This is brought about by a rise in the relative prices of the commodities concerned, as production is extended by the use of less efficient land and more intensive utilisation of more efficient land.[5]   Thus relative prices are governed by demand and by costs, while costs in turn are influenced by technique and by the supply of natural factors of production, and demand is influenced by the distribution of income.

All this differs from orthodox theory in only one respect, but that is an important one.   There is no tendency to

[1] Vol. III, p. 224[19].   [2] Vol. III, p. 228[20].
[3] See below, p. 16.   [4] Vol. III, p. 758[21] and p. 761[22].
[5] Vol. III, p. 733[23] and p. 778[24].   Marx's treatment of rent is more realistic than the usual academic exposition.   He allows for improvements in technique and so has no presumption in favour of diminishing returns to capital (p. 907)[25].   It is interesting to note that he realises how "rent enters into cost of production" for a particular commodity : "the rent of cereal land becomes a determining element in the price of cattle" (p. 892)[26].

II

long-run equilibrium and the average rate of profit is not an equilibrium rate, or a supply price of capital. It is simply an average share in the total surplus which at any moment the capitalist system has succeeded in generating.

As the argument is presented in Volume I it appears on the surface to be very different, but the differences arise from what is omitted rather than from what is included in the analysis. We start from a purely dogmatic statement. " The exchange values of commodities must be capable of being expressed in something common to them all, of which they represent a greater or less quantity. . . . A use-value, or useful article, has value only because human labour in the abstract has been embodied or materialised in it. How, then, is the magnitude of this value to be measured ? Plainly, by the quantity of the value-creating substance, the labour, contained in the article. The quantity of labour, however, is measured by duration, and labour-time in its turn finds its standard in weeks, days, and hours." [1]

The standard of measurement is labour of average quality. " All labour of a higher or more complicated character than average labour is expenditure of labour-power of a more costly kind, labour-power whose production has cost more time and labour,[2] and which therefore

[1] Vol. I, pp. 4-5[(27)].

[2] The excess of a skilled man's wage over an unskilled would be limited by the greater cost of his education, in a world of free mobility and equal opportunity. In reality, the supply of skilled workers (and still more, of professional workers) is restricted by the fact that the families of unskilled workers cannot generally allow their children time for any education at all above the statutory minimum. The extra wages of skilled men, therefore, measure not only their cost of training, but also a scarcity value artificially created by the structure of society. Marx neglected this somewhat obvious point, no doubt because he was anxious to stress the major class conflict between capitalists and workers as a whole, and did not want to complicate the picture by allowing for subsidiary conflicts within each class. See also below, p. 90, n. 2.

has a higher value, than unskilled or simple labour-power.
. . . In every process of creating value, the reduction
of skilled labour to average social labour, *e.g.*, one day
of skilled to six days of unskilled labour, is unavoidable.
We therefore save ourselves a superfluous operation, and
simplify our analysis, by the assumption, that the labour
of the workman employed by the capitalist is unskilled
average labour." [1]

The *value* of a commodity consists not only of the
labour-time directly employed in producing it, but also of
the *value* of the raw materials and plant involved. " The
values of the means of production used up in the process
are preserved, and present themselves afresh as constituent
parts of the value of the product." [2] " The means of production . . . give up to the product that value alone
which they themselves lose as means of production."
The *value* of raw materials, and auxiliary substances such
as fuel, pass immediately into the *value* of the product, while
equipment transfers to the product the *value* which it loses
by wear and tear. [4] The *value* of means of production, in
turn, is derived from the labour-time which is required to
produce them, and " means of production supplied by
Nature without human assistance, such as land, wind,
water, metals in situ, and timber in virgin forests " transfer
no *value* to the product. [5] Thus all *value* is created by labour.

Whatever inward meaning the conception of *value* may
have had for a student of Hegel, to a modern English
reader it is purely a matter of definition. The *value* of a
commodity consists of the labour-time required to produce
it, including the labour-time required by subsidiary commodities which enter into its production.

What is the relationship of *value* to price? At first

[1] Vol. I, pp. 179-80[28].   [2] Vol. I, p. 180[29].   [3] Vol. I, p. 185[30].
[4] Vol. I, pp. 185-6[31].   [5] Vol. I, p. 186[32].

Marx states dogmatically that commodities tend to exchange at prices which correspond to their *values* (so that the ratio of the prices of any group of commodities is the same as the ratio of their *values*). " Price is the money-name of the labour realised in a commodity." [1] Relative prices may differ from relative *values*, as a result of some temporary disturbance in the market, " but these deviations are to be considered as infractions of the laws of exchange of commodities ".[2]

The definition of *value* has to be stretched and strained a good deal in order to make it possible for Marx to maintain that prices tend to correspond to *values*. To create *value*, in Marx's system, labour-time must be socially necessary. The labour-time socially necessary to produce a given output of a commodity may vary for two distinct sets of reasons. If a new labour-saving process is introduced, the socially necessary labour-time embodied in the commodity concerned is reduced, and its *value* consequently falls.[3] But demand also influences *value*. No commodity embodies *value* unless there is a demand for it, and, where there is over-production of a particular commodity, part of the labour embodied in it turns out not to have been necessary to meet the social demand, and the average *value* of the total output of the commodity concerned is consequently reduced.[4] Natural factors of production create no *value*, but it is assumed that the scarcity, for instance, of diamonds, increases the labour-time devoted to searching for them to a sufficient extent to account for their high price.[5] Thus the formulation of Volume I slurs over a number of problems which are clearly distinguished in Volume III.

The main problem, however, Marx does not attempt to

[1] Vol. I, p. 74[33].   [2] Vol. I, p. 136[34].   [3] Vol. I, p. 6[35].
[4] Vol. I, p. 80[36]. Cf. Vol. III, p. 745[37].   [5] Vol. I, p. 7[38].

deal with in Volume I at all.   This concerns the tendency of the rate of profit to equality in different lines of production.   In a system in which prices correspond to *values* the net product of equal quantities of labour is sold for equal quantities of money.   Thus (given uniform money-wage rates) surplus, in terms of money, per unit of labour is everywhere equal.   To say that relative prices correspond to relative *values* is the same thing as to say that the rate of exploitation is equal in all industries.   But if capital per man employed (the organic composition of capital) is different in different industries, while profit per man (the rate of exploitation) is the same, profit per unit of capital must vary inversely with capital per man.   It would be possible for both the rate of profit and the rate of exploitation to be equal in all industries only if the ratio of capital to labour employed were also equal.

In Volume I, Marx leaves this question open.[1]   In Volume III, he shows that capital per man varies with technical conditions, while competition between capitalists tends to establish a uniform rate of profit.   The rate of exploitation therefore cannot be uniform, and relative prices do not correspond to *values*.[2]

Marx entangled himself in an artificial difficulty by starting from the assumption of a uniform rate of exploitation.   There is no warrant for this assumption.   If wages are equal in all industries, surplus per man employed (the

[1] Vol. I, p. 293[(39)].
[2] Vol. III, p. 185[(40)].   In his numerical example Marx calculates the *values* of the commodities produced in the different industries from the average rate of exploitation in industry as a whole.   But the prices of the commodities differ from their *values* in such a way as to make the rates of exploitation actually enjoyed by the capitalists in the different industries vary with the organic composition of their capitals.   As I see it, the conflict between Volume I and Volume III is a conflict between mysticism and common sense.   In Volume III common sense triumphs but must still pay lip-service to mysticism in its verbal formulations.

rate of exploitation) varies with net productivity per man employed, and, in general, productivity per man is greater where capital per man is greater. In Marx's own words : " The prevailing degree of productive power shows itself in the relative preponderance of the constant over the variable capital. . . . If the capital in a certain sphere of production is of a higher composition [than the average] then it expresses a development of the productive power above the average." [1] Thus the rate of exploitation tends to vary with capital per man employed.

The capitalists can be relied upon to see (apart from errors of judgment and perturbations in the market) that they do not increase capital per man employed unless they are assured of a corresponding increase in net profit per man employed, and the very same process which produces an equal rate of profit between industries produces unequal rates of exploitation.

The fact of exploitation makes profit possible, but there is no reason why the *rate* of exploitation should be treated as either logically or historically prior to the rate of profit. Logically, what is important is the total amount of surplus which the capitalist system succeeds in acquiring for the propertied classes, and there is no virtue in dividing that total by the amount of labour employed, to find the rate of exploitation, rather than by the amount of capital, to find the rate of profit. Historically, it is natural to suppose that different industries are developed with widely

[1] Vol. III, p. 881[(41)]. In the preface to Volume III (p. 26) Engels quotes Julius Wolf : " A plus in constant capital has for its premise a plus in the productive power of the labourers. . . . Therefore, if the variable capital remains the same and the constant capital increases, surplus value must also increase." Engels repudiates this view with indignation, and declares it to be directly contrary to Marx's theory. But he merely abuses Wolf, without entering into any argument, and it is impossible to see wherein Wolf's statement differs from the above statement by Marx.

varying rates of exploitation, varying rates of profit, and varying ratios of capital to labour. The push and pull of competition then tends to establish a common rate of profit, so that the various rates of exploitation are forced to levels which offset differences in the ratio of capital to labour. The movement from an equal rate of exploitation towards an equal rate of profit is not a process in the development of capitalism, but a process in the development of economic analysis, from the primitive labour theory of value towards a theory of the interaction between relative demands and relative costs.

According to Marx's own argument, the labour theory of value fails to provide a theory of prices. He used it nevertheless to express certain ideas about the nature of the capitalist system, and the importance of these ideas in no way depends upon the particular terminology in which he chose to set them forth.

First of all, Marx shows that the development of the capitalist system is founded on the existence of a class of workers who have no means to live except by selling their labour-power. Capitalism first expropriates the peasant and the artisan,[1] and then exploits their labour. The possibility of exploitation depends upon the existence of a margin between total net output and the subsistence minimum of the workers.[2] If a worker can produce no more in a day than he is obliged to eat in a day, he is not a potential object of exploitation. This idea is simple, and can be expressed in simple language, without any apparatus of specialised terminology. But it is precisely these simple and fundamental characteristics of capitalism that are lost sight of in the mazes of academic economic analysis.

Next, Marx uses his analytical apparatus to emphasise

[1] Vol. I, Part VIII, " The So-called Primitive Accumulation ".
[2] Vol. I, p. 171[42]; Vol. III, p. 912[43].

the view that only labour is productive.[1]   In itself, this is nothing but a verbal point.   Land and capital produce no *value*, for *value* is the product of labour-time.   But fertile land and efficient machines enhance the productivity of labour in terms of real output, and, indeed, " there is immanent in capital an inclination and constant tendency, to heighten the productiveness of labour ".[2]   Under capitalism " the productiveness of labour is made to ripen, as if in a hot-house ".[3]   Whether we choose to say that capital is productive, or that capital is necessary to make labour productive, is not a matter of much importance.

What is important is to say that *owning* capital is not a productive activity.   The academic economists, by treating capital as productive, used to insinuate the suggestion that capitalists deserve well by society and are fully justified in drawing income from their property.[4]   In the past, a certain superficial plausibility could be given to this point of view by treating property and enterprise as indistinguishable.   But this method of confusing the issue is no longer effective.   Nowadays the divorce between ownership and enterprise is becoming more and more complete, and " the last illusion of the capitalist system, to the effect that capital is the fruit of one's own labour and saving, is thereby destroyed ".[5]   The typical entrepreneur is no longer the bold and tireless business man of Marshall, or the sly and rapacious Moneybags of Marx, but a mass of inert shareholders, indistinguishable from *rentiers*, who employ salaried managers to run their concerns. Nowadays, therefore, it seems simple to say that owning property is not productive, without entering into any logic-chopping disputes as to whether land and capital are productive, and without erecting a special analytical

---

[1] Vol. I, p. 188[(44)]; Vol. III, p. 963[(45)].   [2] Vol. I, p. 309[(46)].
[3] **Vol. I, 641**[(47)].   [4] Cf. Vol. I, p. 443[(48)].   [5] Vol. III, p. 597[(49)].

apparatus in order to make the point.

Indeed, a language which compels us to say that capital (as opposed to ownership of capital) is not productive rather obscures the issue. It is more cogent to say that capital, and the application of science to industry, are immensely productive, and that the institutions of private property, developing into monopoly, are deleterious precisely because they prevent us from having as much capital, and the kind of capital, that we need. This view is inherent in Marx's analysis. He foresaw the time when " the monopoly of capital becomes a fetter upon the mode of production, which has sprung up and flourished along with, and under it. Centralisation of the means of production and socialisation of labour at last reach a point where they become incompatible with their capitalist integument." [1] The substance of Marx's argument is far from being irrelevant to the modern situation, but the argument has become incompatible with its verbal integument.

The increasing productive power of labour under capitalism gives rise to a serious awkwardness in Marx's terminology. His method of measuring output in terms of *value* short-circuits the index-number problem (though it leaves open the problem of assessing labour of different degrees of skill in terms of a unit of " simple labour " [2]). But since real output is an important concept, the problem must be dealt with, and not merely ignored. So long as man-hours of labour, of given intensity, are constant, the total *value* created per unit of time is constant. But, as time goes by, output in real terms is increasing. The *value* of commodities is constantly falling, and, so long as real wages are constant, the *value* of labour-power is also falling. The purchasing power of a given *value* of variable capital over labour-power is therefore increasing. The

[1] Vol. I, p. 789[(50)].   [2] See above, p. 12.

problem of finding a measure of real output — a measure which in the nature of the case must contain a certain arbitrary element — is not solved by reckoning in terms of *value*, for the rate of exchange between *value* and output is constantly altering.

The simplest method of handling Marx's apparatus is to postulate a given money-wage rate per hour. Then if real hourly wages are constant, prices must also be constant (assuming that wage-good prices do not alter relatively to prices in general). As the real output from a given amount of labour-time increases, a constant rate of creation of *value* $(v + s)$ is represented by an increasing total of money, and the *value* of a unit of money is falling. The rising rate of exploitation is then expressed by a constant v and a rising s, in money terms. Alternatively, the *value* of a unit of money may be taken as constant. Money wages and prices are then falling as productivity increases ; $v + s$ is constant, and the rising rate of exploitation is expressed by a fall in v.

The awkwardness of reckoning in terms of *value*, while commodities and labour-power are constantly changing in *value*, accounts for much of the obscurity of Marx's exposition, and none of the important ideas which he expresses in terms of the concept of *value* cannot be better expressed without it.[1]

---

[1] An instructive example of Marx's method of argument is his treatment of commerce (Vol. III, chap. 17[51]). Labour employed in selling commodities, in packing and preparing them for the market, and in book-keeping, creates no *value*. It is merely engaged in realising *value* created in industry. Transport, on the other hand, does create *value* (*loc. cit.* p. 340). The distinction is clearly important. Industry and transport are necessary to society in a sense in which the activity of searching for buyers is not, and in the present age of advertisement the distinction between production costs and selling costs is even more significant than it was in Marx's own day. But Marx creates an unnecessary puzzle for himself by posing the question — What is the source of the wages and profits earned in com-

But the terminology which Marx employs is important because of its suggestive power. No school of economics has ever used a perfectly colourless terminology. Overtones ring in the mind of the reader, even if the writer believes himself to be coldly scientific. Marshall's use of the term *waiting* provides an example of verbal suggestion. He is concerned to show that it is necessary for the owners of wealth to receive interest, in order to overcome the temptation to dissipate their capital in present consumption. It would be natural to draw the moral that if capitalists have to be bribed to keep their capital intact, they ought rather to be expropriated, and their capital put into safe keeping for the benefit of society. But Marshall, while he regards *abstinence* as too strong a term, represents them as performing the service of *waiting*, for which they have a right to be rewarded.[1] Professor Pigou uses the word *exploitation*, highly charged with opprobrious implications, for the difference between real wages under perfectly competitive conditions and under monopoly,[2] so that the reader is unconsciously lulled into the conclusion that, as long as competition prevails, labour receives all

mercial enterprise, and how is the commercial capital preserved, when no *value* and no surplus is directly created by commerce? The industrial capitalist is not interested in acquiring *value*, but in acquiring money, or rather purchasing power over commodities and labour, and he is prepared to pay the commercial capitalist, and, indirectly, the commercial labour, which assists him to realise his surplus — that is, to sell his commodities. The question of the amount of *value* involved is purely formal. If we choose to reckon commercial labour as productive, the total *value* created is so much the greater, and the average *value* of commodities is correspondingly greater, everything else remaining the same. It is obviously somewhat arbitrary where the line is drawn, and the more labour is counted as productive the greater the average *value* of commodities. The choice as to where to draw the line affects nothing except the rate of exchange between *value* and money.

A similar obfuscation of a simple point is to be found in chap. 45 of Volume III on " Absolute Ground-Rent ".

[1] *Principles of Economics*, p. 232. See below, p. 54.
[2] *Economics of Welfare*, Part III, chap. 14.

that it can rightly claim. A hundred instances could be found in academic usage.

Marx was very much alive to the importance of suggestion. He shows how even an algebraical formula is not innocent of political implications. He insists that the rate of exploitation must be written $\frac{s}{v}$, not $\frac{s}{s+v}$. The two formulations express precisely the same situation, but they imply two different attitudes to the capitalist process. The ratio $\frac{s}{v}$ expresses the " real fact " of the " exclusion of the labourer from the product " of his work, while the ratio $\frac{s}{s+v}$ presents the " false semblance of an association, in which labourer and capitalist divide the product in proportion to the different elements which they respectively contribute towards its formation ".[1]

Marx's method of treating profit as " unpaid labour ", and the whole apparatus of constant and variable capital and the rate of exploitation, keep insistently before the mind of the reader a picture of the capitalist process as a system of piracy, preying upon the very life of the workers. His terminology derives its force from the moral indignation with which it is saturated.

I hope that it will become clear, in the following pages, that no point of substance in Marx's argument depends upon the labour theory of value. Voltaire remarked that it is possible to kill a flock of sheep by witchcraft if you give them plenty of arsenic at the same time. The sheep, in this figure, may well stand for the complacent apologists of capitalism ; Marx's penetrating insight and bitter hatred of oppression supply the arsenic, while the labour theory of value provides the incantations.

[1] Vol. I, p. 543[52].

APPENDIX

VALUE IN A SOCIALIST ECONOMY

While abandoning the view that prices correspond to *values* under capitalism, Marx believed that, under socialism, the labour theory of value would come into its own. " Only when production will be under the conscious and prearranged control of society, will society establish a direct relation between the quantity of social labour-time employed in the production of definite articles and the quantity of the demand of society for them. . . . The exchange, or sale, of commodities at their value is the rational way, the natural law of their equilibrium." [1] Following an example to illustrate differential rent, in which 10 quarters of wheat, whose cost, excluding rent, is 240 shillings, are sold for 600 shillings, he writes : " If we imagine that the capitalistic form of society is abolished and society is organised as a conscious and systematic association, then those 10 quarters represent a quantity of independent labour, which is equal to that contained in 240 shillings. In that case society would not buy this product of the soil at two and a half times the labour contained in it. The basis of a class of land owners would thus be destroyed. This would have the same effect as a cheapening of the product to the same amount by foreign imports." [2]

" In the case of socialised production . . . the producers may eventually receive paper cheques, by means of which they withdraw from the social supply of means of consumption a share corresponding to their labour-time." [3]

" After the abolition of the capitalist mode of pro-

[1] Vol. III, p. 221 [(53)].   [2] Vol. III, p. 773 [(54)].   [3] Vol. II, p. 412 [(55)].

23

duction, but with social production still in vogue, the determination of value continues to prevail in such a way that the regulation of the labour time and the distribution of the social labour among the various groups of production, also the keeping of accounts in connection with this, become more essential than ever." [1]

The major point which emerges from these passages is that under socialism income from property will be abolished and each individual will receive a share in the total product corresponding to his own contribution to it. This reflects the substantial meaning of Marx's theory, which can always be expressed without using the concept of *value*. But these passages also imply that, in a rational economic system, prices should be made to correspond to the *values* of commodities.

Can this view be justified? Marx regards depreciation of capital as entering into the *value* of output, and clearly we must include it, for the object of the ideal pricing system is to make the prices of commodities correspond to their costs to society, and wear and tear of plant is a real cost.[2]

In the simplest case, therefore, if all incomes from

[1] Vol. III, p. 992[56]. Marx also makes Robinson Crusoe, the typical economic planner, keep his accounts in terms of average labour-time. Vol. I, p. 48[57].

[2] One passage (Vol. III, pp. 306-8[58]) suggests that Marx did not take this view and that he regarded the correct system as one in which prices are proportional to labour cost, excluding depreciation of equipment. Engels states that this passage was expanded by him from a note in the manuscript, and perhaps some confusion crept in in the process.

Marx conceives of depreciation as equivalent to wear and tear. Depreciation due to the mere passage of time is not a social cost, once the investment has been made, though it must be taken into account in planning new investment. Some investment, for instance the original layout of a railway, has a permanent life, and its use involves no social cost at all, after the initial investment. Capital of this type must be treated, in Marx's system, like land, which adds to real output without adding to *value*.

surplus are abolished, prices would be regulated by wages cost *plus* depreciation.

This would be appropriate if investment has come to an end because no further increase in the stock of capital has any social usefulness, and all income is both derived from and devoted to current consumption. In such a case capital, in orthodox language, has ceased to be a " scarce factor of production ", and the orthodox theory of prices would come to the same thing as the labour theory of value.

What if investment is still being made? Suppose that there is no private saving in the socialist economy, but that investment in new capital equipment is considered desirable [1] and that free services, such as education, are provided to the community. The outlay on investment and free services generates purchasing power in excess of the cost of consumable output. One method of absorbing this excess is to impose an income tax. Prices on average would then be equal to costs, but spendable income would be less than costs. An alternative method is to impose a purchase tax, so that prices exceed costs. How should this tax be assessed ? If prices are to correspond to *values*, in Marx's usual sense, the tax must be proportional to wages cost. The situation would then be the same as the situation with an equal rate of exploitation in each industry, the tax, which provides for investment and free services, appearing as the socialist equivalent of surplus. The tax would be added to labour cost at each stage of production, including maintenance of equipment ; it would therefore enter into the cost to each socialist enter-

---

[1] Under a communist system " society must calculate beforehand how much labour, means of production, and means of subsistence it can utilise without injury for such lines of activity as, for instance, the building of railroads " (Vol. II, p. 361 [59]).

prise of its constant capital—that is, its raw materials and depreciation of equipment. All prices would therefore be raised above costs of production in the same proportion, and the effect would be equivalent to an *ad valorem* tax on the sales of all commodities to final consumers. This would be a reasonable way of assessing the tax (provided that there is no relevant difference between commodities on the demand side) and, so far, *value* appears to be justified as a guide to pricing under socialism.

But, in the foregoing argument it has been tacitly assumed that each industry works under *constant returns*, so that a given proportional increase in outlay produces an equal proportional increase in the output of the commodity concerned. When this condition is not fulfilled the concept of *value* raises a serious difficulty. Let us eliminate the other complications by abstracting from capital, so that wages are the only cost of production, and by assuming that no taxation is necessary to create a fund for investment, and then let us consider Marx's example of producing wheat under conditions of diminishing returns from land.

The problem has two aspects. The first concerns the appropriate intensity of cultivation of pieces of land which differ in quality. The maximum product is obtained by a given number of men employed when the *marginal productivity* of labour — the addition to output caused by employing an additional man — is equal on each piece of land. It would be wasteful to employ the labour in such a way that its average productivity is equal, unless average and marginal productivities happened to be proportional.

Suppose there are two pieces of land on which the conditions shown in the table below obtain. Suppose that 25 men are available. To follow the principle of making the *value* of wheat equal on alpha and beta land

Men Employed	Wheat Produced	Average Output per Man
Alpha Land		
10	100	10
15	120	8
Beta Land		
10	80	8
15	105	7

it would be necessary to allocate 15 men to alpha and 10 to beta. The total product would then be 200, and output per man would be 8 on each piece of land. But a total product of 205 could be obtained by the same men if 15 were allocated to beta and 10 to alpha. The average product would then be greater on alpha than on beta, and the two lots of wheat would differ in *value*. In this case the criterion of *value* fails to give the best results.

The second aspect of the problem concerns the pricing of the wheat. In Marx's example, quoted above, the marginal cost of a quarter of wheat, when 10 quarters are produced, is 60 shillings, and the average cost is 24 shillings. It would be possible to sell the wheat at 24 shillings a quarter, and Marx suggests that this is the correct policy. But it would be more reasonable to argue thus : this product yields a surplus, above its labour cost, of 360 shillings, when it is sold at marginal cost. What is the best use to which this surplus can be put ? To subsidise wheat prices might be the right answer. But, even if wheat ought to be subsidised, there is no particular reason why the best rate of subsidy should be that which just compensates for the difference between marginal and average cost. A smaller or greater rate of subsidy might be preferable. And some other commodity or some different purpose, such as educational services, might have a stronger claim to be subsidised. It would be an unlikely accident that selling the wheat at its average cost would yield the best results.

Thus, to follow the criterion of *value* would lead to avoidable waste and a maldistribution of social resources between different uses.

There remains the question of the allocation of new investment between the various branches of socialised production. If the authorities concerned have a clear idea of the social need for investment in various branches they can allocate investment accordingly, without any guidance from the pricing system. But, when the most obvious needs have been met, it might be convenient to take a leaf out of the capitalist book, and require the socialist enterprises to earn a rate of interest on all capital allotted to them, so as to insure that trivial investment demands of one are not pressed before more urgent demands of another.

If this system is used, the last link with the theory of *value* is broken.

CHAPTER IV

THE LONG-PERIOD THEORY OF EMPLOYMENT

For the most part, Marx conducts his argument upon the assumption that there is no problem of the inducement to capitalists to invest in real capital : " Accumulate, accumulate ! That is Moses and the prophets." [1] The capitalists are not particularly interested in enjoying luxurious expenditure ; [2] they are interested in acquiring more capital, and each is forced by the competitive struggle to enlarge his capital so as to take advantage of new techniques. So long as they have some profits to invest, they can be relied upon to invest them, irrespective of the prospect of profit or the rate of interest. [3] Thus, in the main argument, the problem of effective demand does not arise. This problem is treated separately by Marx, as the problem of " realising surplus value ", and his treatment of it is discussed below. [4]

The problem of unemployment exists, however, even when the problem of effective demand is ruled out. The amount of employment, at any moment, depends upon the amount of capital in existence and the technique of production. As time goes by, capital accumulates and the amount of employment tends to increase. Available

---

[1] Vol. I, p. 606[(60)].   [2] Vol. III, p. 285[(61)].

[3] At one point Marx speaks of a fall in profits reducing accumulation " because the stimulus of gain is blunted " (Vol. I, p. 633[(62)]). But the idea is not followed out, and the rest of the argument is consistent with the fall in accumulation being due merely to the fact that there is less profit available to be invested.

[4] See Chapter VI.

labour also increases, with the natural increase of population and with the advance of capitalism into fresh spheres,
which pours into the labour market a stream of peasants
and artisans deprived of their means of livelihood. There
is normally a fringe of unemployed workers — the reserve
army of labour [1] — and the limit to output is set by full
capacity of capital equipment, not by full employment
of labour.

In these circumstances, the level of real wages is determined by the bargaining power of capitalists as a class and
workers as a class. So long as the workers do not combine
they are helpless, and must take what they can get.[2]
Wages therefore tend to be depressed to the lower limit
set by subsistence level.[3]

Even when wages are at rock-bottom the capitalists still
endeavour to squeeze more profit out of the workers, by
lengthening the working day,[4] screwing up the intensity

---

[1] Vol. I, p. 643 *et seq.*[63].   [2] Vol. I, p. 655[64].

[3] Marx's first formulation of the theory of wages is purely dogmatic.
Labour-power, like other commodities, tends to be sold at its *value*, and
the *value* of labour-power is the labour-time necessary to produce the
means of subsistence of the workers, and of the children who will replace
them (Vol. I, pp. 149-52[65]). This subsistence level contains a " historical
and moral element ", since it partly depends upon the " habits and degree
of comfort in which the class of free labourers has been formed ", that is,
upon the standard of life obtaining before capitalism dispossesses the
peasants and turns them into " free labourers ". This treatment of the
determination of wages, like the dogmatic treatment of prices, is gradually
abandoned as the argument develops. The *value* of labour (subsistence
wages) does not determine the level of wages, but merely describes the
limit below which wages cannot lie for long without reducing the labour-
power of the workers and so threatening to destroy the basis of exploitation.

Marx's reference to a " historical and moral " element in the determination of subsistence wages is often interpreted to mean that the *value*
of labour tends to rise, as capitalism develops, with the customary standard
of life. I find no warrant for this interpretation. And, if it were adopted,
it would reduce Marx's argument to circularity, for it would mean that
the level of real wages determines the *value* of labour-power.

[4] Vol. I, p. 215[66].

of work,[1] and drawing women and children into industry. There is a lower limit, set by starvation level, to the real earnings of a family, but the amount of work which the family is forced to do to earn those wages can be increased by these devices.[2]

This process of extravagant exploitation leads to a reaction. The health of the workers is undermined and the supply of future generations threatened. Enlightened self-interest then compels the capitalists to submit, though reluctantly, to labour legislation, which curbs their own excessive greed. Factory Acts limit the working day and improve conditions of labour, and wages are prevented from falling below subsistence level.[3]

The helpless situation of the workers is due to the industrial reserve army. So long as there is unemployment their bargaining power is chronically weak. The accumulation of capital, however, is going on all the time, and at some periods the stock of capital, which governs the amount of employment offered, catches up upon the supply of labour. Their bargaining position is then strong and real wages tend to rise. Profits consequently fall, and the rate of accumulation is slowed up relatively to the growth of population, so that the reserve army grows again.[4] Meanwhile, the capitalist system, which cannot tolerate low profits, reacts by adopting new techniques which economise labour.[5] Under the stimulus of high wages labour-saving inventions are made, so that a given amount of capital henceforth offers less employment. The reserve army of labour is thus further recruited by technological unemployment. Moreover, there is a fresh motive for extending capitalism into new spheres, and finding new labour to exploit. The temporary bargaining strength of

[1] Vol. I, p. 407[67].　　[2] Vol. I, p. 392[68].　　[3] Vol. I, p. 251[69].
[4] Vol. I, p. 634[70].　　　　　　[5] Vol. I, p. 643[71].

the workers is destroyed by these means, and real wages fall again.[1]

Thus over the long run wages are regulated by the expansion and contraction of the reserve army.[2] The situation which Marx considers most favourable to a rise in wages is an increase in the stock of capital without any change in technical methods or in the ratio of capital to labour. Employment per unit of capital is then constant, and as capital expands employment increases and unemployment alls, so that the scales are gradually tipped in favour of labour.[3] Increasing productivity of labour he does not regard as favourable to rising wages. It is associated with increasing capital per man, so that a given amount of capital offers a falling amount of employment.[4] Moreover, growing mechanisation of industry destroys the demand for skill, and reduces the worker to a mere fragment of a man,[5] so that the lower limit to wages is depressed to a pure subsistence level, including no margin for education.[6]

In one passage Marx admits that a rise in productivity may raise real wages so that the workers obtain some share in the achievements of technical progress,[7] but it seems clear that the argument of *Capital* did not lead him to expect any appreciable upward trend in the level of real wages under capitalism, while the *Communist Manifesto* predicts an actual decline in wages with the development of labour-saving technique.

By and large, events have not fulfilled this prediction, and Marx's argument requires modification if it is to be brought into line with the rise in real wages which has

[1] Marx regards the fall and rise in the reserve army of labour as being of the same nature as the trade cycle (Vol. I, p. 647[72]) ; this point is discussed below, p. 84.
[2] Vol. I, p. 651[73].   [3] Vol. I, p. 631[74].   [4] Vol. I, p. 650[75].
[5] Vol. I, p. 494[76].   [6] Vol. I, p. 362[77].   [7] Vol. I, p. 532[78].

actually occurred in modern times. Marx's contention is that the mechanism of the reserve army of labour keeps wages within limits which permit the continuance of the capitalist system. An increase in productivity raises the upper limit to wages tolerable to capitalism. The development of trade-union power tends to push wages towards that upper limit, while the counteracting force of monopoly prevents them from rising above it.[1] At the same time the incentive to the capitalists to react to a rise in real wages by introducing labour-saving techniques becomes progressively weaker as the proportion of wages cost to capital cost falls.

This modification of Marx's argument impairs the austere simplicity of the original formulation, but it does not affect its moral. It is relevant, for practical purposes, to compare the average standard of life at the present time, not with what it was in 1848, or with what it was in the stone age, but with what it might be now under a more rational economic system.[2] It is the relative, not the absolute, share of labour in total output that is important.

Marx's theory of wages brings into a clear light many points which are often neglected in academic economics. But, as soon as the rigid subsistence-level theory is abandoned, it provides no definite answer to the central question — what determines the division of the total product between capital and labour? The rate of exploitation, the

[1] In Marx's scheme the growth of population provides another counteracting force, since it demands a certain rate of capital accumulation if unemployment is to be kept within bounds.

[2] Those modern Marxists who seek to deny that any rise in real wages has occurred, or to explain it away as solely due to the exploitation of colonial peoples, play into the hands of the conservative trade-union leaders, who look back to their own ragged and barefoot childhood and count up the blessings which capitalism has brought to the workers. It is unnecessary to meet such arguments upon their own ground, since it is easier to cut the ground from under their feet.

division of the working day between paid and unpaid time, the division of real output into wage-goods and other goods — these are all merely alternative ways of formulating the problem of distribution. None provides any clue to finding the answer.

The rate of profit on capital is simply an average share in the total of profits which the system as a whole is producing. The rate of real wages moves, with the varying fortunes of the class struggle, between a lower limit vaguely defined in terms of the subsistence level and an upper limit which is not defined at all. The rate of exploitation, at any moment, is determined by the difference between real wages and total output. But, apart from a general presumption that the rate of exploitation will increase with increasing productivity of labour, there is no law which governs its movement. The academic theory, as we shall see in a moment, is in no better case. If there is any law governing the distribution of income between classes, it still remains to be discovered.

CHAPTER V

THE FALLING RATE OF PROFIT

It was a generally accepted tenet in the orthodox economics of Marx's day that there is a long-run tendency for the rate of profit on capital to fall. Marx accepted this view and set himself to account for the phenomenon of falling profits. His explanation does not turn upon the difficulty of realising surplus value — the problem, as we now say, of a deficiency of effective demand — but is intended to be valid even when that problem does not arise.

He based his explanation upon the rising organic composition of capital.[1] Capital accumulation and technical progress do not necessarily involve an increase in capital per man employed. Inventions may, on balance, reduce capital cost per unit of output as much as labour cost, for they may improve the efficiency of labour in making machines as much as in working machines. This possibility Marx allows for. He shows how " cheapening the elements of constant capital " offsets the tendency of the organic composition of capital to rise.[2] Technical progress may also reduce the period of turnover of capital goods. Chemical processes such as bleaching are speeded up, and the development of transport economises the stocks which it is necessary to hold at each stage of production and marketing.[3] This tends to reduce capital per man employed. Nevertheless, Marx takes the view that there is

---

[1] See above, p. 7.　　　　[2] Vol. III, p. 276[(79)].

[3] Engels makes these points in a chapter which he supplied to fill a gap in the manuscript for Volume III (chap. 4, " The Effect of the Turnover on the Rate of Profit ").

on balance a strong tendency or capital per man to increase as time goes by, and this assumption is a natural one to make.

Marx's law of the falling tendency of profits then consists simply in the tautology: when the rate of exploitation is constant, the rate of profit falls as capital per man increases. Assuming constant periods of turnover, so that $c + v$ measures the stock of capital:[1] when $\frac{s}{v}$ is constant and $\frac{c}{v}$ is rising, $\frac{s}{c + v}$ is falling.[2]

This proposition stands out in startling contradiction to the rest of Marx's argument. For if the rate of exploitation tends to be constant, real wages tend to rise as productivity increases. Labour receives a constant proportion of an increasing total. Marx can only demonstrate a falling tendency in profits by abandoning his argument that real wages tend to be constant. This drastic inconsistency he seems to have overlooked, for when he is discussing the falling tendency of profits he makes no reference to the rising tendency of real wages which it entails.

Orthodox economic theory also contains a law of falling profits. In a given state of knowledge, according to the orthodox argument, output per man rises less than in proportion to capital per man, as capital increases, since a given amount of capital will always be used in the most efficient way that the ruling technique permits, so that additions to capital must be pressed into successively less and less productive uses. Thus the *marginal productivity* of capital — the addition to output due to a unit increase in the stock of capital — falls as capital increases relatively to labour employed. In the orthodox theory the rate of profit is governed by the marginal productivity of capital,

[1] See above, p. 7. [2] Vol. III, p. 247[(80)].

and the rate of profit falls as capital per man increases. But in the orthodox system, competition among employers insures that real wages are equated to the marginal productivity of labour, and the marginal productivity of labour rises as capital per man increases. Thus a falling tendency in profits entails a rising tendency in wages. For the orthodox economists this presents no difficulty, but for Marx it is a stumbling-block.

What happens to the rate of profit if real wages remain constant? With constant real wages, the rate of profit rises or falls, as capital per man increases, according as the ratio of the proportionate increase in product to the proportionate increase in capital exceeds or falls short of the ratio of profits to product. Suppose that the net product is 100 and that profits and wages in the first instance are each equal to 50 so that the ratio of profit to product is $\frac{1}{2}$. Suppose that an increase of capital per man from 100 to 110 leads to an increase in net product from 100 to 108. Then wages remain equal to 50 and profits rise to 58. Thus a 10 per cent increase in the stock of capital leads to a 16 per cent increase in the total of profits, and the rate of profit on capital rises. If the product rose to only 105, when capital per man increased to 110, the rate of profit on capital would be constant. With any lower ratio of increment of product to increment of capital the rate of profit would fall.

An attempt might be made, on this basis, to rescue Marx from his inconsistency by arguing that, in a given state of knowledge, the marginal productivity of capital must be assumed to fall very sharply beyond a certain point. On that assumption, accumulation will lead sooner or later to a falling rate of profit, even when real wages are constant. But it is very unnatural to assume given knowledge in a dynamic system, and, certainly, that

37

assumption is alien to Marx's method, for, in his scheme, an increase in the ratio of capital to labour can only occur as a result of what, in the academic scheme, would be regarded as a change in technical knowledge.[1] If knowledge develops as capital accumulates, there need be no tendency to diminishing returns, and with constant returns there can be no tendency for the rate of profit to fall (always assuming that the problem of effective demand is ruled out). The most that we can say is that periods of falling profits may occur when capital per man increases very rapidly relatively to the rate of advance in technical knowledge. In Marx's view, however, technical knowledge is not an independent factor, and when accumulation is rapid a strong stimulus is applied to labour-saving invention.

Moreover, the whole apparatus of the theory of *value* is designed to exclude the notion of attributing productivity to capital, and allows no room for the concept of the marginal productivity of a particular factor. A theory of falling profits based on the falling marginal productivity of capital would be something quite different from Marx's theory.

Marx's theory, as we have seen, rests on the assumption of a constant rate of exploitation. Certain causes which may lead to a rise in the rate of exploitation he treats as offsetting tendencies.[2] Hours of work may be lengthened (with a constant daily wage) and the intensity of work may be increased, for instance by speeding up machines.[3] Real wages may be reduced,[4] or an increasing amount of labour may be employed in direct services, where both capital per man and real wages are abnormally low.[5] To

[1] See above, p. 8. [2] Vol. III, chap. 14[81].
[3] *Loc. cit.* p. 273[82]. [4] *Loc. cit.* p. 276[83].
[5] *Loc. cit.* pp. 277-8[84]. My analysis of " Disguised Unemployment " (*Essays in the Theory of Employment*) bears a close resemblance to this argument.

these tendencies, which all help to raise the rate of exploitation, there are obvious limits, and Marx argues that
they cannot be sufficiently strong to offset the falling
tendency of the rate of profit. This may be readily
admitted. But the rise in the rate of exploitation which
comes about through a rise in productivity, with constant
hours and intensity of work, and constant real wages, is
not limited in the same way. Productivity may rise without limit, and, if real wages are constant, the rate of exploitation rises with it. Marx appears to have been in some
confusion upon this point, for when he begins to discuss the
effect of a rise in productivity on the rate of exploitation,
he switches over in the middle of the argument to discussing the effect of changing the length of the working
day.[1]

The trouble probably arose, like most of the obscurities
in Marx's argument, from his method of reckoning in
terms of *value*. With given labour-time, of given intensity,
the rate of *value* created is constant. Thus $v + s$ is constant.
It might seem, at the first glance, that $\frac{s}{v}$ can rise only if
wages fall. But this is an illusion. An increase in productivity reduces the *value* of commodities, and the *value*
of labour-power, with constant real wages. Thus v falls

[1] Vol. III, p. 290[(85)] : " To the extent that the development of the
productive power reduces the paid portion of the employed labour, it
raises the surplus-value by raising its rate ; but to the extent that it
reduces the total mass of labour employed by a certain capital, it reduces
the factor of numbers with which the rate of surplus-value is multiplied
in order to calculate its mass. Two labourers, each working 12 hours
daily, cannot produce the same mass of surplus-value as 24 labourers each
working only 2 hours, even if they could live on air and did not have to
work for themselves at all. In this respect, then, the compensation of the
reduction in the number of labourers by means of an intensification of
exploitation has certain impassable limits. It may, for this reason, check
the fall of the rate of profit, but cannot prevent it entirely."

towards zero, and $\frac{s}{v}$ rises towards infinity, and all the time real wages are constant. Alternatively, it might be argued that Marx was unconsciously assuming that increasing productivity does not affect the wage-good industries, so that constant real wages are compatible with a constant rate of exploitation. But, however we interpret it, Marx's argument fails to establish a presumption that the rate of profit tends to fall, when the problem of effective demand is left out of account.

His argument leads him to suppose that a situation might arise in which the total of profits remains constant, while capital continues to accumulate. This he describes as an absolute over-production of capital.[1] If the total of profits is constant, new capital can obtain a share only at the expense of old capital. Cut-throat competition between capitalists sets in, and part of the capital is forced to " lie fallow ".[2] Mr. Kalecki's analysis of the top of a boom[3] bears a certain resemblance to this picture. In Mr. Kalecki's model of the trade cycle the total of profits is a function of the rate of investment. At the turning point of the cycle, the rate of investment is constant from one period to the next. The total of profits is therefore constant. But the stock of capital is increasing. The rate of profit is therefore falling, and it is this fall in the rate of profit which pulls the system down into the slump. In Marx's scheme there is perfect competition, so that part of the capital is used to capacity and part lies idle. In Mr. Kalecki's scheme there is imperfect competition, and the constant total of profit is spread over an increasing amount of capital by a general decline in the utilisation

[1] Vol. III, pp. 294-300[86].
[2] *Loc. cit.* p. 295.
[3] *Essays in the Theory of Economic Fluctuations*, p. 140.

of capital.[1] Apart from this minor difference, the two arguments appear very similar.

But the resemblance is superficial, for in Mr. Kalecki's scheme it is the level of effective demand which regulates the total of profits, while in Marx's scheme the total of profits is unable to increase for some other reason, and, as we have seen, Marx fails to make out his case that the total of profits is limited, apart from effective demand.

It may seem idle to object to Marx's argument, based on a constant rate of exploitation, while at the same time maintaining that the assumption of constant real wages is unrealistic. If the rate of exploitation were in fact constant, and if Marx was right in supposing that technical progress tends to increase capital per man, it might appear that his formula — when $\frac{s}{v}$ is constant and $\frac{c}{v}$ rising, $\frac{s}{c+v}$ is falling — would after all embody an important truth. But the appearance is deceptive. For $\frac{c}{v}$ does not depend solely upon technical conditions, but also upon employment per unit of capital equipment. It may be true that capital per unit of capacity tends to increase, but output per unit of capacity is highly variable. And it varies, not only between boom and slump, but also over the long run. There are always booms and slumps, but in some periods slumps are deeper and longer than in others, so that the average utilisation of capital, good years with bad, tends to be less in some periods than in others. And, with given equipment, the lower is utilisation, the greater is $\frac{c}{v}$. Thus Marx's formula merely shows that, given $\frac{s}{v}$, profits tend to

[1] See below, p. 74.

rise or fall with the state of trade. There needs no ghost come from the grave to tell us this.

In short, it seems that Marx started off on a false scent when he supposed that it was possible to find a law of profits without taking account of the problem of effective demand, and that his explanation of the falling tendency of profits explains nothing at all.

CHAPTER VI

EFFECTIVE DEMAND

So far we have been discussing those parts of Marx's argument which ignore the problem of effective demand — which treat, as he puts it, of the production of surplus value, as opposed to the realisation of surplus value. But he also provides the elements of a theory of effective demand, and lays the basis for a study of the law of motion of capitalism quite different from the law of the falling tendency of profits.

Orthodox economics used to eliminate the problem of effective demand, and justify the assumption of full employment, by appealing to Say's Law. This so-called law consists in the statement that supply creates its own demand, so that an increase in output always generates a sufficient increase in expenditure to clear the market of the commodities produced. This proposition is re-stated in a more sophisticated form by Marshall when he writes, " The whole of a man's income is expended in the purchase of services and of commodities. . . . It is a familiar economic axiom that a man purchases labour and commodities with that portion of his income which he saves just as much as he does with that which he is said to spend." [1] If this view were correct there could be no problem of a deficiency of money demand for any output that could be produced. Until the orthodox axiom was challenged by Mr. Keynes's theory of employment, it was not questioned by the academic economists. Indeed,

[1] *Pure Theory of Domestic Values*, p. 34.

it provided the principal shibboleth which divided the orthodox from heretical theorists such as Hobson and Gesell.

Marx was not deceived by it. " Nothing could be more childish than the dogma, that because every sale is a purchase, and every purchase a sale, therefore the circulation of commodities necessarily implies an equilibrium of sales and purchases. . . No one can sell unless someone else purchases. But no one is forthwith bound to purchase, because he has just sold. . . . If the split between the sale and the purchase become too pronounced, the intimate connection between them, their oneness, asserts itself by producing — a crisis." [1]

To analyse this problem Marx devised a simple and penetrating argument. He divides total output into two groups — capital goods and consumption goods.[2] The output of group I, the capital-good industries, consists of $c_1 + v_1 + s_1$, and the output of group II, the consumption-good industries, consists of $c_2 + v_2 + s_2$. The method can be refined to any extent — for instance group I can be subdivided into raw materials and equipment, and group II into wage goods, mainly consumed by workers and partly by capitalists, and luxury goods consumed only by capitalists. But for the main argument a division into two groups is sufficient.

To simplify the analysis Marx confines it in the first instance to a system in which there is no net investment, so that the whole of output is devoted to current consumption and replacement of pre-existing capital as it wears out. The whole capitalists' net income, as well as wage-income, is then devoted to consumption. Marx regards this assumption as a drastic abstraction from reality, for in reality the main purpose of the capitalists

[1] Vol. I, p. 87[(87)].   [2] Vol. II, p. 457[(88)].

is to apply current surplus to the acquisition of new capital. The assumption is made solely for purposes of exposition.[1]

In a system with zero net investment — simple reproduction in Marx's phrase — the whole output of group I consists of replacement of capital   Thus $c_1 + v_1 + s_1 = c_1 + c_2$. Therefore $v_1 + s_1 = c_2$. The output of group II is equal to wages *plus* capitalists' income. Thus $c_2 + v_2 + s_2 = (v_1 + s_1) + (v_2 + s_2)$. Again it follows that $v_1 + s_1 = c_2$. The net output of group I is balanced by the replacement of capital in group II.[2]

The first problem which Marx solves by this argument is the apparent paradox that total outlay must be equal to total incomes, while in any one industry receipts exceed income-payments by the depreciation of capital.[3] This is the problem which has caused Major Douglas so much anxiety. Marx shows how the payments which represent depreciation from the point of view of group II appear as income for group I.

Next, he shows how even a system of simple reproduction (with zero net investment) is not free from the danger of disequilibrium. The value of c partly consists of amortisation funds attached to long-lived equipment, and these are generally allowed to accumulate over a period of years and are then expended in a single burst when the equipment requires to be renewed. If the age-composition of the stock of equipment is such that renewals are required at a steady rate, equilibrium is not disturbed. If, however, the ages of the machine are not spread evenly, outlay on renewals in some years will exceed, and in some years fall short of the amortisation funds, and equilibrium will be ruptured. When renewals are in excess, $v_1 + s_1$ exceeds c_2 ; the increase in v_1 in turn

---

[1] Vol. II, p. 456[89]. [2] Vol. II, p. 465[90].
[3] Vol. II, p. 473[91]. See also *Marx-Engels Correspondence*, letter No. 67.

increases $v_2 + s_2$ and boom conditions develop. When amortisation funds exceed renewals there is a slump.[1] "Unless a constant proportion between expiring (and about to be renewed) fixed capital and still-continuing (merely transferring the value of its depreciation to its product) fixed capital is assumed . . . the mass of circulating elements [raw materials] to be reproduced in one case would remain the same while the mass of fixed elements to be reproduced would have increased. Therefore the aggregate production of I would have to increase, or, there would be a deficit in the reproduction, even aside from money matters.

"In the other case . . . there would be either a decrease of the aggregate production of I, or a surplus (the same as previously a deficit) which could not be converted into money. . . . I must contract its production, which implies a crisis for its labourers and capitalists, or produce a surplus, which implies another crisis. Such a surplus is not an evil in itself, but it is an evil under the capitalist system of production."[2]

Marx suggests that the fact that the trade cycle has a period of ten years may indicate that the average length of life of plant is ten years.[3] This view (which he throws out merely as a passing hint) cannot be established, for the differences in the length of life of various types of plant must damp down the cycle of renewals, while variations in net investment swamp it altogether, but the idea is interesting since it shows that Marx was on the track of the idea that variations in investment are the key to the trade cycle.[4]

He shows how investment generates boom conditions. "Since elements of productive capital are continually

[1] Vol. II, pp. 543-7[92]. [2] Vol. II, p. 545-6[93]. [3] Vol. II, p. 211[94].
[4] Cf. Robertson, *A Study of Industrial Fluctuations*, p. 36.

46

withdrawn from the market and only an equivalent in money is thrown on the market in their place, the demand of cash payers for products increases without supplying any elements for purchase. Hence a rise in prices, of means of production and of subsistence. To make matters worse, swindling operations are always carried on at this time, involving a transfer of great capitals. A band of speculators, contractors, engineers, lawyers, etc., enrich themselves. They create a strong demand for consumption on the market, wages rising at the same time. . . . In those lines of business in which production may be rapidly increased, such as manufacture proper, mining, etc., the rise in prices causes a sudden expansion, which is soon followed by a collapse. The same effect is produced in the labour-market, where large numbers of the latent relative over-population [the reserve army], and even of employed labourers, are attracted towards the new lines of business." [1]

Marx emphatically rejects the notion that the cycle is a merely monetary phenomenon : " That which appears as a crisis on the money market, is in reality an expression of abnormal conditions in the process of production and reproduction ".[2]

Two further suggestions of great interest are made in the course of the argument. First, that boom conditions in the home country lead to an excess of imports over exports, while a deficiency of home investment may be balanced by a surplus of exports ; [3] second, that gold mining, which generates " purchases without sales ", has an effect upon activity similar to investment.[4]

Unfortunately, Marx did not complete the manuscripts which deal with net investment (reproduction on an

[1] Vol. II, p. 362[95].   [2] Vol. II, p. 365[96].
[3] Vol. II, p. 362[97] and p. 546[98].   [4] Vol. II, p. 549[99].

enlarged scale) [1] and this part of the work degenerates into a mere jumble of notes. The main idea, however, is clear enough. Part of the surplus of both group I and group II is saved, that is, not expended on the products of group II (consumption goods) ; $v_I + s_I$ then exceeds c_2, and must be matched by an equivalent outlay on new capital goods out of s_2. Saving represents sales without purchases, and can proceed smoothly only if it is offset by equivalent investment — purchases without sales. Such a balance is possible, as he shows in a series of numerical examples, but " a balance is an accident under the crude conditions of [capitalist] production ".[2] The cause of crises is to be sought in a lack of balance, which is an ever-present threat to the stability of the system. Marx does not develop a full theory of the trade cycle, or of the long-run movement of capitalism, but he points the direction in which a theory can be found.

He rejected the crude under-consumption theory current in his day,[3] but his own analysis clearly leads to the view that maldistribution of consuming power is the root of the trouble. Engels found the following note, inserted for future elaboration, in the passage (referred to above) which describes an investment boom : " Contradiction in the capitalist mode of production : the labourers as buyers of commodities are important for the market. But as sellers of their own commodity — labour-power — capitalist society tends to depress them to the lowest price. Further contradiction : The epochs in which capitalist production exerts all its forces are always periods of overproduction, because the forces of production can never be utilised to such a degree that more value is not only pro-

[1] Vol. II, chap. 21, " Accumulation and Reproduction on an Enlarged Scale ". See Engels' preface, Vol. II, p. 11.
[2] Vol. II, p. 578[(100)].   [3] Vol. II, p. 476[(101)].

duced but also realised ; but the sale of commodities, the realisation on the commodity-capital, and thus on the surplus value, is limited, not by the consumptive demand of society in general, but by the consumptive demand of a society in which the majority are poor and must always remain poor." [1]

This note, combined with the equations of reproduction, suggests that Marx intended to work out a theory on some such lines as this : consumption by the workers is limited by their poverty, while consumption by the capitalists is limited by the greed for capital which causes them to accumulate wealth rather than to enjoy luxury. The demand for consumption goods (the product of group II) is thus restricted. But if the output of the consumption-good industries is limited by the market, the demand for capital goods (group I) is in turn restricted, for the constant capital of the consumption-good industries will not expand fast enough to absorb the potential output of the capital-good industries. Thus the distribution of income, between wages and surplus, is such as to set up a chronic tendency for a lack of balance between the two groups of industries.

Some hints of this line of thought are to be found in Volume III. " The conditions of direct exploitation and those of the realising of surplus-value are not identical. They are separated logically as well as by time and space. The first are only limited by the productive power of society, the last by the proportional relations of the various lines of production and the consuming power of society. This last-named power is not determined either by the absolute productive power nor by the absolute consuming power, but by the consuming power based on antagonistic conditions of distribution, which reduce the consumption

[1] Vol. II, p. 363[102].

of the great mass of the population to a variable minimum within more or less narrow limits. The consuming power is furthermore restricted by the tendency to accumulation, the greed for an expansion of capital. . . . To the extent that the productive power develops, it finds itself at variance with the narrow basis on which the conditions of consumption rest." [1] " The last cause of all real crises always remains the poverty and restricted consumption of the masses as compared to the tendency of capitalist production to develop the productive forces in such a way, that only the absolute power of consumption of the entire society would be their limit." [2]

To work out a theory on these lines it is necessary to deal with the problem of the inducement to invest. If capitalists were always prepared to invest their surplus in capital goods, without regard to the prospect of profit, the output of capital goods would fill the gap between consumption and maximum potential output. The balance between the two groups of industries would be self-adjusting, and crises would not occur, however wretched the level of consumption. (Though fluctuations in the reserve army of labour, owing to the interplay of capital accumulation and technical progress, would not be eliminated.) Thus to clinch the argument it is necessary to show that investment depends upon the rate of profit, and that the rate of profit depends, in the last resort, upon consuming power. It is necessary, in short, to supply a theory of the rate of profit based on the principle of effective demand.

This Marx fails to do, for he had meanwhile worked out his theory of the falling tendency of profit, based on the principle of the rising organic composition of capital. In Volume III this theory is inextricably mixed up with

[1] Vol. III, pp. 286-7[103].   [2] Vol. III, p. 568[104].

the under-consumption theory, and the two lines of thought are not brought into any clear relation with each other. The theory of the falling rate of profit is a red herring across the trail, and prevented Marx from running the theory of effective demand to earth.

Marx evidently failed to realise how much the orthodox theory stands and falls with Say's Law, and set himself the task of discovering a theory of crises which would apply to a world in which Say's Law was fulfilled, as well as the theory which arises when Say's Law is exploded. This dualism implants confusion in Marx's own argument, and, still more, in the arguments of his successors.

CHAPTER VII

THE ORTHODOX THEORY OF PROFIT

THE most striking difference between Marx and the orthodox economists appears in the conception of surplus. To
Marx, depreciation and wages are the only necessary costs
of production, and rent, interest and profit are all sub-
divisions of surplus. In the orthodox system, rent of land
is a surplus, because land is a " free gift of nature ", and
would exist just as much if no payment were made for
it, but interest and profits are the necessary supply price
for capital, without which it would not be forthcoming.
Wages, interest and profit are grouped together as " the
reward of human efforts and sacrifices ". Thus attention
is distracted from the distinction between income from
work and income from property, and a moral justification
is provided for interest and profit.

In order to build up a theory based on the notion of
the supply price of capital, academic economics developed
a highly artificial method of analysis. All relevant conditions except the stock of capital — consumers' demands,
the supply of labour and of natural resources and knowledge of technical methods of production — are taken as
given, and the stock of capital is conceived to adjust itself
in such a way as to establish equilibrium with the given
conditions.

The rate of profit earned by a given stock of capital is
governed by its marginal productivity — the addition to
output caused by making a small unit addition to capital.
Any given stock of capital is conceived to be used in the

most efficient manner that existing knowledge permits. It follows from this, as we have seen,[1] that an increase in capital, relatively to other factors of production, leads to a fall in its marginal productivity. The rate of profit thus depends upon the relative scarcity of capital, and falls as the stock of capital increases.

In Marx's system the stock of capital in existence at any moment determines the amount of labour employed. In the orthodox system full employment of the available labour is achieved, in equilibrium, whatever the stock of capital. There are a number of alternative ways of producing a given output, with different combinations of factors, even when the state of knowledge is assumed constant, and producers are conceived to substitute one factor for another in response to changes in their relative prices, so that a given output is always produced at minimum cost, while consumers substitute one commodity for another, so that the maximum satisfaction is obtained from a given outlay. Thus a change in relative factor prices alters both the combination of factors used in producing a given commodity and the relative outputs of commodities requiring different combinations of factors. The relative prices of the factors of production are conceived to settle, in equilibrium, at the level at which all are fully employed.

The principle of substitution plays an important, perhaps an exaggerated, part in academic economics, and it was one of the main refinements of analytical technique introduced by the generation which succeeded Marx. By him it is completely neglected. He assumes that, with given technical knowledge, there is only one possible combination of labour with capital in each industry, and he pays no attention to substitution by consumers.

This makes his analysis appear somewhat primitive.

[1] See p. 36.

On the other hand, he does pay attention to the reaction of changes in the supplies of factors on technical knowledge itself. And technological unemployment — the reserve army of labour — is one of the central mechanisms, in his system, which regulates the relative earnings of the factors of production. The orthodox system treats a change in technical knowledge as an arbitrary shift in the position of equilibrium. Unemployment, certainly, may result from the change ; but it is regarded as temporary, and attention is concentrated upon the position of equilibrium appropriate to the new technique of production, in which labour will once more be fully employed. Thus in the orthodox scheme technological unemployment appears hazily at the fringe of a field of vision focused on the point of equilibrium, while Marx focuses upon the industrial reserve army, and leaves the principle of substitution in the haze.

These divergences, however, are of minor importance compared to the complete difference of outlook between Marx and the orthodox economists on the question of the supply of capital.

To Marx, the desire to own capital does not have to be explained, and, so long as any profit at all is obtainable, the capitalists not only preserve what wealth they have, but accumulate, accumulate. In the orthodox system, owners of wealth " discount the future ", so that if the return on capital falls below a certain level, they feel that it is not worth while to continue to own it, and devour it in present expenditure. Thus the rate of interest is the *reward of waiting* — the reward of not consuming one's capital,[1] while the excess of profit (net of depreciation)

[1] *Waiting*, which means owning capital, is sometimes confused with saving, which means acquiring capital by refraining from consuming current income. In the first edition of Marshall's *Principles* there is no

over the interest on a secure loan is the *reward of risk-bearing*. These together make up the supply price of capital, and the stock of capital is in equilibrium, tending neither to increase nor diminish, when the rate of profit is equal to the supply price of the existing stock of capital.

Marx's analysis is too simple, but the orthodox theory is too far-fetched. The notion of " discounting the future " is not based upon direct observation, but arises from the desire to represent owning wealth as a " sacrifice ". It is logically self-consistent, but has little bearing on reality. A full theory of accumulation would no doubt be very complicated, and it is possible to argue that " discounting the future " should play some part in it. But it can easily be seen that that part must be a minor one. For in a world in which it was predominant there would be no problem of unemployment. As soon as unemployment appeared in such a world, it would only be necessary to lower the rate of interest. Owners of wealth would then increase their expenditure (present pleasures being preferred at the lower rate of return on *waiting*). A boom

confusion : " That surplus benefit which a person gets in the long run by postponing enjoyment, and which is measured by the rate of interest (subject as we have seen to certain conditions), is the reward of *waiting*. He may have obtained the *de facto* possession of property by inheritance or by any other means, moral or immoral, legal or illegal. But if, having the power to consume that property in immediate gratifications, he chooses to put it in such a form as to afford him deferred gratifications, then any superiority there may be in deferred gratification over those immediate ones is the reward of his waiting. When he lends out the wealth on a secure loan the net payment which he received for the use of the wealth may be regarded as affording a numerical measure of that reward." [Footnote] ". . . it is perhaps best to say that there are three factors of production, land, labour and the sacrifice involved in waiting " (Book VII, chap. vii, p. 614). Here Marshall clearly regards *waiting* as simply owning capital. In later editions this passage was dropped. In other passages, *e.g.* seventh edition, Book IV, chap. vii, § 8, p. 233, *waiting* appears to imply saving, and the argument becomes extremely obscure.

in the luxury industries would develop, investment to increase their capacity would become profitable, and (allowing time for labour to move from one industry to another) unemployment would disappear. Poverty and social injustice would remain, but unemployment could be no more than a passing accident.

It would be hard to maintain that this picture corresponds to reality, and that all the disasters of unemployment are due to some impediment which prevents the rate of interest from falling fast enough and far enough to fend them off. Professor Cassel,[1] indeed, has maintained something of the sort. But his argument was directed to proving the " necessity of interest ", and as soon as we transfer it to the context of the problem of unemployment, its lack of plausibility becomes glaringly obvious. Certainly the existence of the rate of interest tends to limit the supply of capital (this point will be discussed in the next chapter), but the rate of interest cannot be identified with the necessary supply price of *waiting*.

To examine the notion of net profit as the supply price of *risk-bearing* it is necessary to distinguish between two ways of using the apparatus of equilibrium analysis. One method is to take the assumption of static conditions literally. If demands for commodities, techniques of production and supplies of labour and natural resources remain unchanged for long enough to allow the stock of capital to be adjusted to them, static equilibrium is established, and, once it is established, nothing alters, and to-day is a mere repetition of yesterday.

In such conditions, all industries would settle down to routine and there would be no scope for enterprise and innovation. There would then be no function for the entrepreneur to perform, and it is argued, for instance by

[1] *The Nature and Necessity of Interest*, p. 148.

Wicksell,[1] that the earnings of the entrepreneur would sink to the level of a manager's salary. Capital would earn no more than the rate of interest, and net profit would disappear, for if an individual " could obtain a share of the product merely in his capacity of entrepreneur . . . everybody would rush to obtain such an easily earned income ".[2] But this argument does not hold water. The mere fact that an entrepreneur performs no useful function is not a sufficient guarantee that he receives no income. If publicans took no part whatever in running their houses it does not follow that competition would eliminate the commission on selling beer, for competition is limited by the number of licences which the authorities choose to issue. In industry, the licence to take part in the pursuit of profit consists in owning some capital, or commanding some credit, with which to make a start. Competition could eliminate net profit only if there was complete freedom of entry into industry, and freedom of entry is not entailed by the postulate of static conditions.[3] It requires either that any individual can borrow indefinite amounts of capital at the ruling rate of interest (a situation which is certainly not to be found in reality), or that production can be carried on in units requiring minute quantities of capital. Wicksell's argument can be plausibly applied to some lines, such as cotton weaving or retail trade, where the skilled worker has a chance to become a small capitalist, though even in these trades the threshold of capital is too high for the unskilled worker to cross. But such trades are nowadays the exception, and even where they survive they are retreating before the advance of large-scale enterprise. Modern technique, as Marx pointed out, fosters the con-

[1] *Lectures*, Vol. I, p. 126.   [2] Wicksell, *loc. cit.*
[3] Wicksell himself points out (*op. cit.* p. 132) that his theory does not apply where monopoly exists.

centration of capital, and the level of profits is supported by a scarcity of enterprise which is not due to the real cost of *risk-bearing*, but to the scarcity of individuals who have anything to risk.

The property qualification for entry into industry differs considerably between different lines of activity, and if the static world is imagined to contain the same technical methods and the same inequality of wealth as are found in reality, its industries must be imagined to stand in a hierarchy, the level of profits being higher where entry is more difficult. Large capitals would be found in the trades enjoying a high rate of profit, while small capitals would be crowded into the low-profit trades.

Marx, like Wicksell, neglects the hierarchy of profits and uses the simplifying assumption that the rate of profit tends to equality in all lines of activity, but in his hands it is a simplification of an entirely different order from that employed by Wicksell to show that profits are not only uniform, but uniformly zero. For Wicksell is abstracting from the most characteristic feature of the capitalist system, while Marx is merely abstracting from certain differences between one industry and another.[1]

The hierarchy of profits consists of the levels of profits, in different industries, which are just not high enough to attract new competition. In dynamic conditions profits stand above their level in the hierarchy during the period of expansion of new industries, and stand below it when an industry is over-expanded relatively to demand (a situation which may persist for indefinitely long periods, since the level of profits at which capital, once invested, is driven out of an industry is often much lower than the level at which new competition is attracted in). A census of profits, taken at any particular moment, would show

[1] Cf. above, p. 2.

many industries out of place in the hierarchy, while the average level of profits departs from the equilibrium level whenever the total stock of capital is changing.

The static method of analysis is legitimate when it is used to point out, by contrast, what is the behaviour of profit in a dynamic world. But often it is used rather to suggest that, as net profit would disappear in equilibrium, it does not very much matter, and can safely be neglected in the analysis of distribution. This kind of argument would be beside the point even if it were correct on its own ground. For dynamic development, as Marx clearly saw, is inherent in the capitalist system, and a static world would be entirely different from the actual world of capitalism in the most fundamental respects. The analysis of static conditions, if taken literally, is no more interesting than speculations as to what life would be like on the moon.

Marshall does not fall into the absurdity of taking the static assumptions literally. He uses the conception of equilibrium merely as an analytical device. At any moment there is a certain equilibrium position towards which the system is tending, but the position of equilibrium shifts faster than the system can move towards any one position of equilibrium. Thus uncertainty is kept alive and the cost of *risk-bearing* enters into the equilibrium supply price of capital.[1]

This analysis is a somewhat awkward cross between static and dynamic theory. But it has more serious defects than lack of elegance. In Marshall's system more risky industries require a higher equilibrium level of profit than steady industries. This, in itself, is a merit of his theory, for it obviously corresponds to something in reality. But

[1] Cf. Pigou, *Economics of Welfare*, Appendix I : " Uncertainty-bearing as a Factor of Production ".

it obscures the influence upon profits of the property qualifications which limit entry into industry, and serves to distract attention (like Wicksell's theory, though by a different method) from the most essential characteristics of the profit system.

Moreover, the notion of the cost of *risk-bearing* as an element in the supply price of capital is, at best, distressingly vague. First, it applies, not to actual profits, but to expected profits. In a world which is stable on the whole, though uncertain in detail, some definite relationship between actual present profits and expected future profits might be established, but in unsettled times the relationship is so complicated and erratic as to defy analysis. Any number of equally plausible hypotheses can be made about it, and, indeed, the " reaction on business confidence " has become a *deus ex machina* which enables economists to prove whatever they please. Second, reluctance to expose wealth to risk is essentially subjective, and there is no method to discover the laws of its operation, except by begging the question, and using the actual level of profits to measure the cost of *risk-bearing*. Third, the subjective element in the supply price of capital must obviously be influenced very much by the past experience of capitalists, so that the level of profits which they feel to be sufficiently attractive to justify enterprise is largely based on a conventional view of what it is reasonable to expect.

But this is not the worst. Even if we could form a clear conception of the equilibrium rate of profit, it would be irrelevant to the actual world. The equilibrium rate of profit is that rate which induces zero net investment. But over the course of history, since the Industrial Revolution began, net investment has always been going on. The actual rate of profit, therefore, good years with bad, has exceeded the equilibrium rate. Abnormal profits are the normal rule.

Moreover, the experience of the inter-war period suggests that the whole competitive *laisser-faire* system is adapted to a strong upward trend in capital accumulation. If capital is not accumulating over the long run, disinvestment in the slump must offset investment in the boom, and to judge by the experience of the nineteen-thirties, the competitive system could not survive a series of slumps of the magnitude induced by negative net investment. Beggar-my-neighbour devices and monopoly schemes, designed to protect the interests of one country or one industry at the expense of the rest, and expansionist policies, New Deals and Experiments, designed to increase activity on the whole, drastically modify the operation of *laisser faire* ; while any attempt to limit the depth of slumps by reducing the inequalities of income must entail still more fundamental changes in the profit system.

The whole apparatus of equilibrium theory therefore seems to be without application to reality. The Marshallian method of analysis is based on the analogy of the pursuit curve. The man on the bicycle is the moving long-period position of equilibrium. The short-period situation follows the path of the dog running after him. But the resources of mathematics fail us if the dog is liable to bite through the tyres of the bicycle when the man slows down his pace.

If the orthodox notion of a definite supply price of capital thus disintegrates upon examination, we are left with nothing but Marx's notion that capital is accumulated and maintained because capitalists are forced to accumulate in order to survive. The lack of a clear treatment of the inducement to invest is, as we have seen,[1] a

[1] See p. 50.

weakness in his treatment of crises, but from a long-period point of view it may well be that it is unimportant, and that any prospective level of profit, within very wide limits, is sufficient to keep the system running. Mr. Keynes puts forward this view, though in more kindly language than Marx : " Most, probably, of our decisions to do something positive, the full consequences of which will be drawn out over many days to come, can only be taken as a result of animal spirits — of a spontaneous urge to action rather than inaction, and not as the outcome of a weighted average of quantitative benefits multiplied by quantitative probabilities. Enterprise only pretends to itself to be mainly actuated by the statements in its own prospectus, however candid and sincere. Only a little more than an expedition to the South Pole, is it based on an exact calculation of benefits to come." [1] " It is not necessary . . . that the game should be played for such high stakes as at present. Much lower stakes will serve the purpose equally well, as soon as the players are accustomed to them." [2]

Thus, with the notion of the supply price of capital, the moral justification of profit as a necessary cost of production disappears, and the whole structure of the orthodox apology falls to the ground.

[1] *General Theory of Employment, Interest and Money*, pp. 161-2.
[2] *Ibid.* p. 374.

CHAPTER VIII

THE GENERAL THEORY OF EMPLOYMENT

So far we have considered the orthodox theory of long-period equilibrium — the theory which applies to a situation in which the stock of capital is adjusted to circumstances, with zero net investment. The process of adjusting the stock of capital to any change in circumstances takes a long time to work through. It is therefore necessary to supplement the long-period theory by an analysis of the short-period situation, in which the process of accumulation is going on.

The orthodox short-period theory was never very precisely stated,[1] but its main outline seems to have been as follows : at any moment the rate of profit is determined by the marginal productivity of the stock of capital in existence. At the rate of interest corresponding to that rate of profit there is a certain rate of saving which the community is willing to undertake, and it is the rate of saving which governs the rate of increase in the stock of capital.[2]

The controversies which have developed in recent

[1] Cf. Keynes, *General Theory*, p. 195.

[2] On this capital theory of the rate of interest Marshall superimposes a monetary theory, by which an *increase* in the stock of gold *lowers* the rate of interest. But the part played by the stock of gold, at any moment, in influencing the level of the rate of interest he does not discuss. (" Evidence before the Gold-Silver Commission ", *Official Papers*, pp. 23, 38, 130.) The failure to reduce these two theories of the rate of interest to a consistent system has been a fruitful source of confusion amongst Marshall's successors. Cf. *General Theory*, p. 183.

years around this theory turn on its application to the problem of unemployment. But in the orthodox scheme the theory of employment scarcely existed, and in its original setting the chief use to which the argument was put was to justify the unequal distribution of income. Unequal distribution is favourable to saving, since it concentrates large incomes in the hands of a few individuals who can saturate their demands for consumption and accumulate wealth without any uncomfortable tightening of the belt. Thus any assault upon inequality, for instance by heavily progressive taxation, is held to be dangerous to society, since it dries up the source of capital accumulation and so prevents economic progress.[1]

This argument is somewhat sophistical, even on its own ground. If society is conceived to be presented with the choice between a more and less equal distribution of income, with a correspondingly lower or higher rate of capital accumulation, it is clear that, by choosing the higher rate of accumulation, society throws the burden of abstinence, not upon the individuals who actually do the saving and enjoy the consequent possession of wealth, but upon the individuals whose income would have been larger if distribution had been more equal. There is therefore a strong presumption that too great a burden of abstinence will be imposed upon the mass of the population — those who enjoy the benefit bearing no part of the cost. It was, indeed, argued that, in the long run, the poor gain from the saving of the rich, since accumulation raises productivity and the general standard of life. But no one would praise the prudence of a man who

---

[1] Cf. my " Economist's Sermon " (*Essays*). Marshall did not take this view, but held, on the contrary, that a measure of redistribution " made quietly and without disturbance " might actually promote the growth of material wealth. *Principles* (seventh edition), p. 230.

ruined the health of his children by starvation in order to bequeath a fortune to his grandchildren.

Moreover, if society is conceived to tolerate inequality in order to promote saving, it is obvious that a large part of the higher incomes runs to waste in providing the rich with a luxurious standard of life. Unequal distribution of income is an excessively uneconomic method of getting the necessary saving done. The argument that inequality is justified because it promotes saving turns inside out, and becomes an argument in favour of corporate saving by the state combined with an egalitarian distribution of consuming power.

But an attack upon the orthodox position has recently developed from quite a different quarter. Mr. Keynes, in his *General Theory of Employment, Interest and Money*, challenged the view, taken completely for granted in the orthodox scheme, that saving promotes accumulation of capital.

He points out that the theory that the rate of saving governs the rate of accumulation depends upon the assumption of full employment. If full employment is guaranteed, investment in real capital cannot increase unless consumption declines, so as to release labour for the investment industries. And every decline in consumption must be offset by an increase in investment to absorb the labour released. The rate of investment is then governed by the desire of the community to save. But the guarantee of full employment is to be found in the orthodox theory, not in the actual working of the capitalist system. A theory which leaves no room for unemployment cannot claim to be relevant to the modern world, even if it was relevant (which is disputable) to an earlier stage in the development of capitalism.

In Mr. Keynes's scheme the rate of investment depends,

not upon the amount of saving which the community wishes to perform, but upon the view which the entrepreneurs take of the profitability of new capital, compared to the rate of interest which they have to pay on borrowed funds. When entrepreneurs decide, for whatever reason, to increase the rate of investment, activity is increased and income consequently rises. An increase in income normally leads to an increase in consumption by the community which is less than the initial increase in income, so that saving rises with income. It is the rate of investment which governs the rate of saving, and not *vice versa*. An increase in the desire to save shows itself, in the first instance, in a reduction in outlay on consumption goods. This reduces income, so that the increased saving fails to materialise. At the same time the profitability of the consumption-good industries is reduced, so that the rate of investment is more likely to decline than to increase. In short, saving, though it is a necessary condition for capital accumulation, is not a sufficient condition.

This argument is in line with Marx's analysis of reproduction in terms of the balance between the consumption-good and capital-good industries, and develops the theory for which he laid the foundation. In particular, Marx's contention that the excess of surplus value over capitalists' consumption (the rate of saving) is limited by the sum of outlay on new capital goods (home investment), the excess of exports over imports (foreign investment) and production of gold,[1] is reinforced by Mr. Keynes's argument. Many refinements and complications (for instance, the effect of working-class saving, of unemployment pay and of government borrowing), neglected by Marx, are elaborated in the Keynesian theory, but the main outline is clearly to be seen in Marx's analysis of investment as

[1] See above, p. 47.

" purchases without sales ", and saving as " sales without purchases ".

The consequences of Mr. Keynes's attack upon ortho-doxy are very far-reaching. First, it cuts the ground from under the pretended justification of inequality, and allows us to see the monstrous absurdity of our social system with a fresh eye.

Next, it shows that there is no automatic self-adjusting mechanism in the *laisser-faire* system which tends to pre-serve full employment. According to one strand of thought, in the orthodox doctrine, this mechanism is provided by the free play of bargaining in the labour market. Any individual can always get work by offering himself at a lower wage than that ruling in the market ; wages measure the *disutility* of labour [1] and if the workers as a whole choose to stand out for a level of wages at which they are not all employed, the consequent unemployment is " voluntary ", and cannot be regarded, properly speaking, as unemploy-ment at all.[2] This argument, in Mr. Keynes's view, is based on the fallacy of composition. It does not follow that, because any individual can obtain employment by cutting wages, the workers as a whole are able to do so. This question is discussed in Chapter X below.

According to a second strand in the orthodox doctrine a self-righting mechanism is provided by the rate of interest. At any moment there is a certain gap between the total income corresponding to full employment and the total of consumption. If full employment is to be achieved, this gap must be filled by investment. In the orthodox scheme, the rate of interest is determined by the interaction of the supply of saving coming from the community with the demand for saving coming from the entrepreneurs making investment, so that the rate of

[1] Cf. above, p. 2.   [2] *General Theory*, p. 16.

interest tends to find the level at which entrepreneurs are willing to undertake a sufficient rate of investment to fill the gap. But Mr. Keynes shows that, if the rate of interest fails to balance investment with saving, in such a way as to give full employment, saving will be balanced to investment by the failure of activity to reach the level of full employment. Thus the process of equalising saving with investment does not provide any guarantee of full employment.

The orthodox theory is trying to solve two variables with only one equation. Mr. Keynes supplies the missing equation by showing how the rate of interest depends upon the supply and demand for money. Though Marx pays no attention to the monetary analysis of the rate of interest it is not incompatible with his system. He opposed to the orthodox " Quantity Theory of Money " (the theory that the level of prices tends to vary with the quantity of money in circulation) the view that the quantity of money in circulation is determined by the demand for it — that is by business habits, the state of activity and the level of prices.[1] The difference between the quantity of money in circulation and the quantity in existence is absorbed in " hoards ". When the demand for money in circulation increases, hoards are reduced.[2] In this Mr. Keynes agrees exactly with Marx. According to Mr. Keynes's analysis a rise in the demand for money in the active circulation raises the rate of interest, and so induces owners of wealth who were holding money to transfer into interest-bearing securities, thus releasing part of their hoards of money for the active circulation.

Marx does not discuss the relationship between hoarding and the rate of interest. He regards interest merely as a mechanism by which surplus is shared between the

Vol. I, pp. 92-9[105].   [2] Vol. I, p. 111[10].

rentier and the active capitalist. In his view, it is impossible to make any generalisation about the behaviour of the rate of interest [1] — it is arbitrarily determined by the push and pull of bargaining strength between lenders and borrowers — and he attaches no importance to its reaction upon other factors in economic life.

In general, according to Mr. Keynes, the rate of interest tends to fall when activity is low, and the demand for money in the active circulation is reduced. It thus tends to reduce the inducement to save and increase the inducement to invest when employment falls off. Conversely it tends to rise when activity is high. Thus some force still remains in the orthodox theory of the rate of interest as a regulator of the economic system.[2] On this basis a new defence of the orthodox position has been erected which amalgamates the two lines of thought referred to above. So long as there is unemployment, on this view, money wages tend to fall, and the fall in wages reduces the demand for money, and so lowers the rate of interest. Thus it is possible to find a sense in which it is formally true to say that unemployment tends to bring about its own cure.[3]

But, in general, the modern tendency in academic theory is to attach little importance to the influence of the rate of interest on employment. On the one hand, it is pointed out that the long-term rate of interest appears to vary very little with movements in employment.[4] On the other hand, even when it does move, its influence upon the inducement to invest is confined to the sphere of housing and public utilities, where long-lived capital is

[1] Vol. III, p. 426[(107)].

[2] Cf. my *Introduction to the Theory of Employment*, p. 82.

[3] Cf. Pigou, " Money Wages in Relation to Unemployment ", *Economic Journal*, March 1938, p. 136.

Kalecki, *Essays*, p. 114.

faced with a comparatively stable demand. In other spheres, the obsolescence of plant is so rapid, and demand so chancy, that investment will be made only when prospective gross returns very much exceed the rate of interest, so that even a large proportionate change in the rate of interest has a negligible influence on the inducement to invest. Thus the rate of interest, though its movements tell in the right direction, is too weak an influence adequately to regulate the level of investment.

The reaction of the rate of interest on the inducement to save has always been problematical. The orthodox theory could still be partially justified if it were possible to show that saving is highly sensitive to changes in the rate of interest. But this thread, as we have already seen, is too weak to support the whole weight of the orthodox argument.[1]

In the modern academic view, therefore, it seems that the importance of the rate of interest was very much exaggerated in the traditional theory, and that Marx was after all not much at fault in neglecting it altogether.

Mr. Keynes's criticism of the orthodox theory was primarily concerned with the problem of unemployment in its short-period aspect, but incidentally it destroys the basis of the long period theory of the supply price of capital. In his scheme, the rate of interest appears as an obstacle to accumulation. For a capital good to exist, in the *laisser-faire* system, it is necessary for it to earn a profit at least as great as can be obtained by lending at interest a sum of money equal to its cost. Capital must, therefore, remain scarce enough to earn the necessary profit, and the higher is the rate of interest the scarcer capital must be. Thus a high rate of interest (for what its influence is worth) not only retards accumulation in the short run, but reduces

[1] See p. 56.

the stock of capital in the long run. Mr. Keynes perhaps exaggerates the ease with which the authorities can control the complex of interest rates (though British experience during and after the war provides a striking confirmation of his views), but, in any case, it is clear that the lower the authorities succeed in setting the rate of interest, the larger the stock of capital is likely to be. Thus the notion of the rate of interest as an element in the necessary supply price of capital is deprived of its foundation.

The long-period extension of Mr. Keynes's theory brings the problem of the reserve army of labour into the foreground of the picture. The propensity to save and the rate of investment determine the level of real output, at any moment. As time goes by, the productivity of labour increases and the amount of employment corresponding to a given level output declines. Thus the technique of production plays an important part in determining the level of employment.

Finally, Mr. Keynes justifies Marx's intuition that the chronic conflict between productive and consumptive power is the root cause of crises. The maldistribution of income restricts consumption, and so increases the rate of investment required to maintain prosperity, while at the same time it narrows the field of profitable investment, by restricting the demand for the consumption goods which capital can produce. Geographical discoveries and technical inventions open alternative fields for investment, while wars from time to time absorb huge quantities of capital. Indeed, the survival of the capitalist system bears witness to the fact that long periods of rapid accumulation can occur. But their recurrence is at the best of times uncertain, and when the stimulus to investment flags, the underlying contradiction between the capacity to produce and the capacity to consume comes to the surface in waste and misery, which becomes more and more intolerable as their causes become more clear. Mr. Keynes's theory gives strong support to Marx's contention that " the real barrier of capitalist production is capital itself ".[1]

Marxist economists have on the whole tended to gloss over the under-consumption element in Marx's theory, and Rosa Luxemburg, who developed it most clearly, is generally regarded as heretical. Under-consumption theories have been associated with an appeal for reform rather than revolution — with the view that capitalism *might* be made to work satisfactorily — and for this reason they are uncongenial to the Marxist creed.

The association of under-consumption theory with a desire to preserve freedom of enterprise and a distaste for revolution is once more exemplified in Mr. Keynes, who regards his own theory as " moderately conservative in its implications ",[2] and finds the philosophy of Gesell more sympathetic than the philosophy of Marx.[3] But this association is superficial, for the maldistribution of income is quite as deeply imbedded in the capitalist system as Marx believed the tendency to falling profits to be, and cannot be eliminated without drastic changes in the system. The case for revolution, as opposed to reform, might have been argued just as well on the basis of the analysis in Volume II of *Capital* as on the basis of Volume III.

[1] Vol. III, p. 293[(108)].   [2] *General Theory*, p. 377.   [3] *Ibid.* p. 355.

CHAPTER IX

IMPERFECT COMPETITION

THE experience of slump conditions in the inter-war period, which gave rise to Mr. Keynes's theory of employment, also led to drastic modifications in the orthodox theory of prices.

The orthodox theory is based upon the assumption of perfect competition. Under perfect competition no individual producer can affect the price of his commodity by altering his rate of output. Each producer is conceived to maximise his profits by producing such a rate of output that marginal cost to him is equal to price — marginal cost being defined as the addition to total costs caused by a small unit increase in the rate of output. In the short period, with given capital equipment, marginal cost is equal to marginal prime cost — the addition to outlay on wages, raw materials, power and wear and tear entailed by a small unit addition to output. Thus price, at any moment, is equal to marginal prime cost, and the excess of receipts over total prime costs, which provides for overhead costs and net profits, is equal to marginal *minus* average prime cost, multiplied by output.

Now, in the general run of manufacturing industry, prime cost begins to rise sharply, as output expands, only when the full capacity output of the plant is approached. It follows that, with perfect competition, any firm which is working at less than full capacity output must be losing the whole of its overhead costs, and can have no motive

for continuing production.[1]   Thus, under perfect competition the rule must be : full capacity output or no
output at all.   But, in reality, full capacity working is a
rarity, even in times of average prosperity, while slump
conditions normally lead to a reduction in the rate of
output from all plant, rather than a complete cessation
of production from some plants, side by side with full
capacity working for the rest.   It appears therefore that,
in reality, perfect competition in selling commodities
cannot be the rule, and that the excess of price over prime
cost cannot be accounted for solely by the difference between marginal and average prime cost.

To meet this difficulty a new type of analysis was
developed.   In this it is assumed that the individual producer is not faced by a price for his commodity over which
he has no influence, but, on the contrary, that an increase
in his output can be sold only if he lowers his price, or
undertakes greater selling costs, for advertisement and the
like.   The sacrifice in price required to make a small
increase in his rate of output saleable (neglecting selling
costs) is represented as depending upon the elasticity of
demand for his particular product, that is, the ratio of the
proportionate change in his sales to the proportionate
change in price.   His profits are maximised when price is
equal to marginal cost multiplied by $\frac{e}{e-1}$, where e is the
elasticity of demand for his product.   For instance, if e is
equal to 3 (the proportionate increase in sales is three
times the proportionate fall in price), price exceeds
marginal cost by 50 per cent.   This provides an explanation of the excess of price over prime cost which does not

---

[1] Marshall was aware of this difficulty, and to solve it he called in
imperfect competition under the guise of " fear of spoiling the market "
(*Principles*, seventh edition, p. 375).

depend upon a difference between marginal and average prime cost.

Imperfection in the labour market has to be considered, as well as imperfection in the market for selling commodities. In the orthodox analysis of perfect competition each individual employer is conceived to be faced by a given wage rate, independent of the amount of labour which he employs, since the amount of employment he offers is too small a proportion of the whole to affect the wage rate. He is conceived to offer employment up to the point at which the marginal productivity of labour (the addition to value of output made by employing one more man) would fall below the wage if any more men were employed. Marginal productivity is thus equated to the wage.

This picture of perfect competition in the labour market is even further from reality than perfect competition in selling commodities. Where labour is unorganised each employer is likely to be faced with a group of workers who have few or no alternatives to working for him, so that they are obliged to take what wage he offers, while to attract labour from further afield he would have to offer a higher wage. It is then to his interest to proceed upon the principles of monopsony (monopoly buying) and confine his offer of employment to the workers who can be had most cheaply, when due account is taken of their efficiency.

Where collective bargaining is the rule, wages are fixed by agreement for the trade as a whole, and each employer may be conceived to take on that number of men which will equate marginal productivity to the wage, according to the rules of competition. But we still have to reckon with the over-all monopsony of employers as a class, which is no less important to-day than when Adam Smith observed that " Masters are always and everywhere in a sort of tacit, but constant and uniform, combination, not to raise the wages of labour above their actual rate ".[1] The marginal productivity of labour to the individual employer tends to be greater than the wage whenever, in order to press employment to the point at which marginal productivity is reduced to equality with the wage, it would be necessary to bid for labour against other employers — " a most unpopular action, and a sort of reproach to a master among his neighbours and equals ".

According to this analysis, the main influence upon the share of labour in the total product is the degree of imperfection of competition in selling commodities and in buying labour. At each stage of production, from the raw-material industry to the retail shop, the seller takes a rake-off on prime cost, governed by the elasticity of demand in that market, and the rake-off at one stage enters into prime cost at the next.

In the market for consumers' goods a relatively small number of sellers face a large number of buyers, so that the imperfection of competition tells in favour of the sellers. In the labour market the position is reversed. Thus the share of labour in total output is ground between the upper and the nether millstones of monopoly and monopsony.

This account of the matter bears a close resemblance to the theory of Lexis, quoted by Engels in the preface to Volume III of *Capital*.[2] " The capitalist sellers, such as the producer of raw materials, the manufacturer, the wholesale dealer, the retail dealer, all make a profit on their transactions, each selling his product at a higher price than the purchase price, each adding a certain percentage to the price paid by him. The labourer alone is unable to raise the price of his commodity, he is com-

[1] *Wealth of Nations*, chap. viii.   [2] Vol. III, pp. 19-20.

pelled, by his oppressed condition, to sell his labour to the capitalist at a price corresponding to its cost of production, that is to say, for the means of his subsistence. . . . Therefore the capitalist additions to the prices strike the labourer with full force and result in a transfer of a part of the value of the total produce to the capitalist class." Engels gives (though grudgingly) his approval to this formulation which, he says, " amounts to the same thing as the Marxian theory of surplus-value ". Lexis thus provides a bridge between Marx and the modern theory.

But while there is a certain moral affinity between the modern theory and Marx's analysis,[1] formally they are quite different. For in Marx's scheme under-capacity working is impossible and the limit to the output of any concern is set, not by the imperfection of the market, but by the capacity of capital. The modern theory exposes many relatively minor defects in capitalism which Marx, concentrating on major issues, was content to ignore.

The theory is good enough for purposes of a general discussion of the nature of the system. But its foundations are too shaky to bear a superstructure of exact analysis. For the economist $\dfrac{e}{e-1}$ is a magical formula, but for the business man the elasticity of demand for his product is

[1] It is curious to observe the transmutation of the notion of " exploitation " which takes place under the influence of the modern theory. In the orthodox scheme labour is " exploited " when (owing to the influence of monopoly) it receives less than the wage which would rule under perfect competition (see p. 21 above). In Marx's scheme labour is exploited to the extent that capital earns a net return. In the modern scheme the whole, not only of interest and net profit, but also of overhead costs, is, in a formal sense, a monopoly profit, and therefore, in the orthodox sense, is the result of exploitation, though some part of it covers necessary costs of production. Moral and analytical considerations thus become inextricably confused. The trouble arises from attempting to apply the criterion of perfect competition to a world in which it is never found in its pure textbook form.

at best a very vague conception. It can only be discovered by trial and error, by instinct or by guess-work. Trial and error are dangerous. Trial may involve a price-cut which will debauch consumers and " spoil the market " by leading to resentment when price is raised again. Error involves loss. When times are not too bad, the business man is content to let well alone. Instinct and guess-work probably teach him no more than to do the same as other people. The gross profit margin, or rake-off on prime cost, therefore, probably depends very much upon historical accident or upon conventional views among business men as to what is reasonable. And any conventional pattern of behaviour which establishes itself amongst an imperfectly competitive group provides a stable result. So long as all adhere to the same set of conventions each can enjoy his share of the market, and each can imagine that he is acting according to the strict rules of competition, though in fact the group as a whole, by unconscious collusion, are imposing a mild degree of monopoly upon the market.

The gross profit margin, however it is determined, can always be expressed in terms of the formula $\dfrac{e}{e-1}$. For instance, if, in a certain case, price is found to be equal to prime cost *plus* 50 per cent of prime cost, we may say that the producer concerned acts as though he believed the elasticity of demand in his market to be equal to 3. But, by saying so, we add nothing whatever to our knowledge of how the gross margin is determined.

The foregoing argument applies to the general run of more or less competitive industry. Where outright monopoly rules, or where a group of commodities is produced by a few powerful firms, there is great scope for individual variations in policy, and it is hard to make any generalisation at all as to what governs the margin of profit per unit of output.

All this makes a serious breach in the smooth surface of the orthodox theory of value, and it seems that economic science has not yet solved its first problem — what determines the price of a commodity?

In his first statement of the theory of value Marshall wrote : " The great central law of economic science " is that " producers, each governed under the sway of free competition by calculations of his own interest, will endeavour so to regulate the amount of any commodity which is produced for a given market, during a given period, that this amount shall be just capable on the average of finding purchasers at a remunerative price ",[1] a remunerative price being defined so as to allow for *normal* profits on capital. This statement may be taken to mean two quite different things. It may mean that each producer, governed by calculations of his own interest, endeavours to maximise the profit, at each moment, on his current rate of output, by balancing marginal cost against marginal gain. This interpretation has been pursued to its logical conclusion by the modern academic economists, and the pursuit, as we have seen, has left us bogged in the conventional gross margin.

The other interpretation is that each producer endeavours to fix, not the price which maximises his current profit, but the price which will be remunerative in the long run. This at first sight seems plausible, but it entirely begs the question of *normal* profits, on which, as we have seen, academic economics fails to provide any theory which is relevant to the real world. Moreover, even if the question of *normal* profits were settled, it would still remain to inquire what level of utilisation of equipment is *normal*

[1] *Pure Theory of Domestic Values*, p. 3.

in the long run. Generally speaking, the lower the level of utilisation, good years with bad, the higher the gross margin required to bring in any given level of profits. But the higher the gross margin, other things equal, the lower the level of utilisation, for, given the expected fluctuations in demand, the amount of capital seeking employment in the industry is governed by the gross margin established in the market. And the amount of capital employed influences the average utilisation per unit of capital. The three determinants, profit per unit of output, profit per unit of capital, and capital per unit of output, are all interdependent, and the whole analysis dissolves in a haze of doubt.

Marx's assumption that capital is always used to capacity cuts through the tangle. But his analysis, as we have seen, yields no more than the theory that the share of labour in output depends upon bargaining power. The Marxian degree of exploitation and the academic formula $\frac{e}{e-1}$ each provides merely a summary method of representing the result of all the various forces that are at work upon the distribution of the product between labour and capital. Neither is an independent force in itself, and neither yields any simple and coherent law of distribution.

Yet an empirical law of distribution is better established than most economic generalisations. In a wide variety of times and places statisticians have found a remarkable constancy in the proportionate share of labour in output as a whole.[1] The variations which both the academic economists and Marx would expect *a priori*, between boom and slump, and over the long run with technical change, fail to appear in the figures.

[1] The evidence for Great Britain and U.S.A. is summarised by Mr. Kalecki, *Essays*, pp. 14-18.

The Marxian theory might yield the explanation that the development of trade-union power has been just sufficiently rapid to prevent the rate of exploitation from rising with the productivity of labour,[1] while the academic theory suggests that a secular rise in monopoly has been just offset by a relative fall in raw-material prices.[2] Both explanations are somewhat lame, and the mystery of the constant relative shares remains as a reproach to theoretical economics.

[1] Cf. above, p. 33.　　　　　[2] Kalecki, *Essays*, p. 33.

CHAPTER X

REAL AND MONEY WAGES

MODERN developments in academic economics, as we have seen, move away from traditional orthodoxy towards Marx. But in one sphere the movement has been in the opposite direction. On the question of the relationship of changes in money wages to changes in real wages, and of changes in real wages to changes in employment, Marx and the orthodox stand together, opposed to the modern theory.

Generally speaking, in the orthodox system, it was taken for granted, without much thought, that a rise in money-wage rates, brought about by a bargain between employers and employed, entails a more or less commensurate rise in real-wage rates,[1] and that a rise in real wages causes a decrease in employment. In any one industry the workers obtain a higher real wage when their money wage rises, for even if the product of the industry is consumed by the workers, a rise in its price, following the rise in its wages cost, will make only a small reduction in the purchasing power of money, so that the workers in that industry gain, while the countervailing loss is thinly spread over the rest of the community. Again, in a single country, an all-round rise in money wages, even if it is accompanied by an equivalent rise in home prices, leaves the prices of imported goods unchanged in the first instance, and so leads to some rise in real wages in the home country. The orthodox economists seem to have pushed the inquiry no

[1] See Pigou, " Real and Money Wage Rates in Relation to Unemployment ", *Economic Journal,* September 1937, p. 405.

further than this, and appear never to have posed the question : What happens when there is an all-round rise in money wages in a closed system without international trade ?

There is no doubt what their answer ought to have been. On the orthodox assumptions of perfect competition, marginal prime cost is equal to marginal wages cost in a closed system. An equal proportional rise in all money wages must therefore lead to the same proportional rise in the level of prices of a given rate of output. It follows that, unless something happens to alter the rate of output, real wages remain unchanged when money wages rise. But this proposition is not to be found in the orthodox writings. On the contrary, it was always assumed that the money-wage bargain determines the real wage, and it was not until Mr. Keynes challenged this assumption that any discussion of the problem was undertaken at all.[1]

A rise in real wages was conceived to reduce output in the short period (though here the argument was excessively vague), while in the long run it was conceived to encourage the substitution of capital for labour, and so to reduce employment per unit of output. Thus it was held that trade unions, by refusing to accept a wage equivalent to the marginal product of the total labour force, may cause a part of it to be unemployed, and so upset the natural self-righting mechanism of the *laisser-faire* system, which was believed to ensure full employment in the absence of interference.

Marx goes even further than the orthodox economists, for he argues explicitly that a rise in money wages has no effect upon the general level of prices. "In the case

---

[1] The challenge was taken up by Professor Pigou (*The Theory of Unemployment*, p. 101) but his later treatment of the subject (*Employment and Equilibrium*) is substantially the same as that of Mr. Keynes.

of a general rise of wages, the price of the produced commodities rises in lines of business where the variable capital predominates, but falls, on the other hand, in lines where the constant, or eventually the fixed, capital predominates." [1]

It is essential to Marx's argument that the rise in wages which comes about when the reserve army falls low and the bargaining position of the workers is strong should be a rise in real wages, not merely a rise in money wages offset by a rise in prices. As we have seen,[2] he maintains that there is a tendency for the reserve army of labour to contract and expand cyclicly. When the stock of capital is large, relatively to the supply of labour, the margin of unemployment is reduced and wages rise. The rise in wages reduces surplus, and slows up the rate of accumulation. The reserve army (which is fed by the natural increase of population and by the opening up of new fields for capitalist exploitation) then has time to grow, relatively to the stock of capital, while labour-saving inventions reduce the amount of employment offered by a given stock of capital. Unemployment is thus increased, and wages fall again. This cycle Marx identifies with the decennial trade cycle.[3]

This identification is an error. The crisis of the trade

[1] Vol. II, p. 393[109]. Here Marx is evidently thinking in long-period terms. His view is that, when wages rise, prices in the first instance remain unchanged (see below, p. 86) so that profits fall by the amount by which wages rise. Thus the rate of profit falls most in those industries where wages cost is the highest proportion of total costs. These industries therefore contract, while industries where profits are relatively raised expand. Prices therefore rise in the first group of industries, and fall in the second, until the rate of profit is restored to equality throughout industry at a new, lower, level. If this interpretation is correct, the whole argument is based on assuming what it requires to prove. It elaborates the consequences of a rise in real wages, but does nothing to show that real wages will rise.

[2] See p. 32.   [3] Vol. I, p. 646[110].

cycle is marked by a decline in total output, but there is no point in Marx's cycle at which output declines. In his scheme the total of output is determined by the stock of capital; the problem of realising surplus does not arise, there is no question of a deficiency of effective demand, and in this part of Marx's argument Say's Law holds undisputed sway. When real wages rise, the rate of accumulation of capital (which is governed by the amount of surplus) is slowed up, but the total of output, wage goods and capital goods together, does not decline. If technique remains unchanged, the total of employment also is maintained, though a relative increase in available labour is taking place; while, with inventions, a gradual fall in the total of employment may take place, as old machines are replaced by new ones which require less labour to produce a given output. This is something quite different from the trade cycle. The difference arises because, in Marx's scheme, the decline in the rate of accumulation is due to a decline in the fund from which savings are made, not from a slackening of the inducement to invest.[1]

There may be in reality a cycle of the type which Marx analyses. But if so, it must be of much longer period than the decennial trade cycle (which he himself, in a different context, connects with the rate of investment[2]), since it depends upon changes in the stock of capital, and in the composition of the capital stock, and these changes must be slow relatively to the changes in the rate of investment, which mark the trade cycle. The operation of Marx's long-period cycle has not been detected by the statisticians,

---

[1] As was noted above (p. 29, n. 3), Marx writes in this context " accumulation slackens in consequence of the rise in the price of labour, because stimulus of gain is blunted ". But this reference to the inducement to invest is an aberration from the rest of the argument, and must be regarded as an isolated example of common sense breaking in.

[2] See above, p. 46.

for, if it exists, it is swamped by the more violent movements of the trade cycle, and disturbed by bursts of invention, due to the progress of science, as well as by wars, geographical discoveries and other large-scale accidents, which are not directly connected with the scarcity of labour, or which, at any rate, cannot be reduced to a simple relationship with it.

The confusion between this long-run cycle, which might be found in a world subject to Say's Law, and the short-run cycle of effective demand, accounts for the ambiguity of Marx's attitude to the problem of under-consumption. Part of the time he is accepting Say's Law and part rejecting it. Push in the Say's Law stop, and effective demand is dominant — the poverty of the workers is then seen to be the last cause of all real crises. Does it follow that a crisis would be relieved by increasing the consuming power of the workers? Pull out the Say's Law stop, and the answer is no. With a given total output, increased real wages means lower profits, and lower profits — push back the stop again — mean crisis.

When Marx is concerned to show that a change in money wages alters, not the level of prices, but the rate of exploitation, he appears to contradict his own argument that a rise in real wages must cause a decline in output.

" In consequence of a rise in wages, especially the demand of the labourers for the necessities of life will rise. In a lesser degree their demand for articles of luxury will increase, or the demand will be developed for things which did not generally belong to the scope of their consumption. The sudden and increased demand for the necessities of life will doubtless raise their prices momentarily. As a result, a greater portion of the social capital will be invested in the production of the necessaries of life, and a smaller portion in the production of articles of luxury, since these fall in price on account of the decrease in surplus-value and the consequent decrease in the demand of the capitalists for these articles. And to the extent that the labourers themselves buy articles of luxury, the rise in their wages — to this degree — does not promote an increase in the prices of necessities of life, but simply fills the place of the buyers of luxuries. More luxuries than before are consumed by labourers, and relatively fewer by capitalists. That is all. After some fluctuations, the value of the circulating commodities is the same as before." [1]

Here there is no reference to the demand for investment goods, but clearly Marx envisages investment continuing, to the extent that the decline in surplus allows, for he talks of new capital being deflected from luxury to wage-good industries. To complete the picture, he ought to show that the output of capital goods, as well as of luxuries, falls off with the fall in surplus. But the fall in capitalist outlay   on luxuries and capital goods together — is exactly balanced by the increase in workers' outlay, and there is no suggestion that the rise in real wages reduces the total of output. This line of argument is consistent with his long-run theory of fluctuations in the industrial reserve army, precisely because, both in this argument and in the theory of the reserve army, the problem of effective demand is ruled out, and Say's Law is in force. For the same reason it is inconsistent with the theory that a rise in wages precipitates a crisis.

Marx was aware of the argument that an all-round rise in money wages (in a closed system) merely raises prices, and leaves real wages unchanged. But he provides a very feeble answer to it. " If it were in the power of capitalist producers to raise the prices of their commodities at will,

[1] Vol. II, p. 391 (III).

they could and would do so without waiting for a rise in wages." [1]   It would be just as convincing to argue that a rise in the price of raw cotton has no effect upon the price of yarn.   Under competitive conditions no one producer can raise his price, unless all the rest do the same.   But if costs are raised for all, all can raise their prices together. Marx goes on : " The capitalist class would never resist the trade unions, since the capitalists could always . . . avail themselves of every rise in wages to raise prices much higher and thus pocket greater profits ". [2]   This argument neglects the conflict of interests between capitalists.   Each benefits by a rise in the wages paid by his rivals, and loses by a rise in the wages which he must pay himself.   Each group has an interest in resisting the particular trade union with which it has to bargain, and it does not follow from the fact that each separately has an interest in low wages that all collectively suffer from a rise in wages.

To a generation brought up under the shadow of the " vicious spiral " of wages and prices, Marx's view that a rise in money wages leaves prices unchanged appears flatly contrary to common sense.   It is easy, however, to understand how he was led to adopt it.   The view that a rise in wages causes a corresponding rise in prices was being used to show that the wage bargain cannot influence real wages and that consequently " trade unions have a *harmful* effect ". [3]   Marx therefore had a strong motive for advocating the view that wages do not influence prices, and as this was the current orthodox opinion, he had no difficulty in accepting it.

Since his day the position has been reversed.   In the

---

[1] Vol. II, p. 392 [112].   The same argument is put forward in *Value, Price and Profit*.

[2] Vol. II, p. 392 [113].

[3] *Marx-Engels Correspondence*, letter No. 83.

year 1930 it was the opponents of trade-unionism who were maintaining that the chief cause of the slump was the obstinate refusal of the workers to accept a cut in wages. If a rise in wages does not raise prices, a fall will not reduce them. A cut in costs will increase profits, and set the wheels of industrial activity revolving again. To this view Mr. Keynes opposed the argument that a cut in wages would waste itself in a fall in prices, and he holds that the trade unions " are instinctively more reasonable economists than the classical school " [1] since they resist wage cuts with whatever power slump conditions leave at their command. It is impossible to imagine Marx reading the Addenda to the Macmillan Report on Finance and Industry and finding Professor Gregory more sympathetic than Mr. Keynes.

But the question cannot be settled by sympathy, and an exact analysis of the effect of a change in money wages on employment is extremely complicated. Under perfect competition an equal proportional change in all wages (in a closed system) must lead to the same proportional change in the level of prices of a given output. But in reality perfect competition does not prevail, and a change in wages may alter the ratio of prices to prime costs. Many prices fail to react immediately to a change in wages cost and this is generally true of house rents, which play a very important part in determining the real value of the money wage. It seems reasonable to suppose, therefore, that a rise in money wages will normally lead to some rise in real wages, at least for a certain time after it occurs. [2]

But the next step in the orthodox argument is by no

[1] *General Theory*, p. 14.

[2] The introduction of trade unions, where none were before, is likely to have an important effect in raising real wages, by squeezing out monopsony profit. This effect depends upon the introduction of a " common rule " (see above, p. 76. Cf. my *Economics of Imperfect Competition*, p. 295).

means obvious. Wages are more fully spent than profits, and a transfer of purchasing power from capitalists to workers stimulates the demand for consumption goods and so tends to increase employment.[1] It may be argued, against this, that the inducement to invest would be reduced by a rise in wages, so that employment in the investment-good industries would decline. This is likely to be true of house-building, where an expansion of demand, due to higher real wages, is unlikely to offset the effect of higher costs, and it may be true of other types of long-lived equipment. On the other hand, investment in equipment for the wage-good industries is likely to be stimulated.

A further complication is introduced by the effect of a rise in prices on the distribution of total profits between *rentiers* and entrepreneurs.[2] A rise of prices reduces the burden of debts fixed in terms of money, and this may tend to stimulate investment.[3] On the other hand, *rentier* incomes are more fully spent than net profits, which include the corporate savings of firms, so that a redistribution of real total profits unfavourable to *rentiers* may tend to restrict consumption.[4] The effect of the redistribution on employment may therefore tell in either direction.

The argument is thus not very conclusive, but it serves to show, at least, that the view, held both by Marx and the orthodox economists, that a rise in wages necessarily causes a fall in employment, cannot be maintained.

[1] Cf. Kalecki, *Essays*, p. 84.

[2] Marx habitually treats capitalists as a single class, and emphasises the conflict between them and the workers. Mr. Keynes's argument reveals a subsidiary conflict between *rentiers* and entrepreneurs, in which the workers side with the entrepreneurs. This conflict comes clearly to the surface in conditions of hyper-inflation and, to a smaller extent, under war-time inflation, when the fixed-income classes suffer relatively more than any other section of the community.

[3] See Kalecki, *Essays*, p. 106.   [4] *Ibid.* p. 87.

The relationship between the Keynesian and the Marxian view of wages is curious. Marx, with the orthodox economists, holds that a rise in money wages causes a rise in real wages, and that a rise in real wages causes unemployment. Mr. Keynes holds that a rise in money wages has little effect upon real wages, but that a rise in real wages tends to increase employment. Both agree that a rise in money wages would be of little use at a time of crisis, Marx because he holds that it will raise real wages, Mr. Keynes because he holds that it will not. But they completely disagree as to the effect of a fall in money wages in a crisis. Marx holds that it brings temporary relief, and enables expansion to be resumed " within capitalistic limits ",[1] while Mr. Keynes holds that it can do nothing but harm. The matter can be finally settled only by detailed statistical investigation, but in the nineteen-thirties the crude test of experience seemed certainly to be on Mr. Keynes's side, and many were then disillusioned who formerly believed in a cut in wages as a cure for slump conditions.

[1] Vol. III, p. 299[(114)].

CHAPTER XI

DYNAMIC ANALYSIS

THE foregoing argument has left a trail of questions to which neither Marx nor the academic economists, ancient or modern, provide satisfactory answers, and the impression which it gives of the present state of economic knowledge is not encouraging. It has generally been the fate of economic theory to run a losing race against the course of history, and never to have completed the analysis of one phase of economic development before another takes its place. It seems likely enough that the same fate will be fulfilled once more. But, if time allows, the questions ought to be answered.

The outstanding questions may be divided into two groups : those which concern the division of the social product, and those which concern the size of the product. To the first group belongs the question of the profit margin on which, as we have seen, modern theory is highly agnostic, as well as the complex question of the relationship between real and money wages.

These problems are formidable, but they might yield to a combination of field investigation and statistical study. The divorce between theory and realistic investigation, which is a standing reproach to academic economics, has been due in the main to the preoccupation of the theorists with propositions about equilibrium conditions, on which, in the nature of the case, evidence from the real world can throw no light at all. There are already signs that, when the theorists begin to ask answerable questions, the statisticians need not despair of finding the answers.

If the problem of the profit margin could be solved, it would isolate one major influence upon the distribution of the social income between classes, and would prepare the way for an investigation of the factors governing the rate of profit on capital. It may be, however, that the mystery of the constant relative shares will not yield to this type of analysis, and that a totally new method is required for its solution.

Questions concerning the total of output may be grouped under two heads — potential production and effective demand. The first is governed by the supplies of the factors of production, and by technique. The study of supplies of natural resources and of labour involves the whole problem of Imperialism, on which the hints thrown out by Marx have been elaborated by later Marxists, and which requires to be reviewed in the light of modern analysis. The study of the supply of capital involves theoretical problems which impinge upon each of our unsolved questions. The overthrow of the orthodox notion of an equilibrium supply price of capital leaves a huge gap in our analysis, and it seems vain to attempt to fill it with an alternative abstract theory. The problem must rather be approached, as Marx approached it, in terms of history — the stock of capital at any moment is the result of developments in the immediate and the remote past, and the stock of capital in existence is an important factor in the determination of its own rate of growth.

Technical knowledge, in academic theory, is usually treated as an arbitrary datum, but Marx is clearly right in arguing that it is largely influenced by the relationship between the supply of labour and the supply of capital. Here, again, an historical approach is the most promising. The influence upon technique of factor prices — the rate of interest and the level of real wages, — elaborated in the orthodox theory, must also be studied by realistic methods.

Problems of effective demand may be examined under the Keynesian categories of the propensity to consume and the inducement to invest. On the first, the main influence is the distribution of income, but there are other elements also in the problem, and the whole natural history of consumers' demand requires to be studied.

The inducement to invest involves the problem of the rate of interest. We need to know, first, how the complex of interest rates reacts to various circumstances and various policies, and, second, how investment reacts to changes in interest. The true balance between the orthodox exaggeration of the importance of the rate of interest and Marx's complete neglect of it can only be struck by realistic investigation.

The problem of indebtedness and the relationship between a concern's own capital and its outside borrowing is also involved in the problem of the inducement to invest, and the legal framework and financial practice in various countries has an important influence on it. Most important of all, the relationship between current and expected profit, and the relationship between expected profits and the inducement to invest, must be established. Here the statisticians meet with a formidable difficulty, for an increase in the rate of investment both causes and is caused by an increase in the rate of profit, so that the evidence is hard, perhaps impossible, to disentangle. Expectations about the future introduce a subjective element into the causation of investment which cannot be ruled out, or reduced to simple objective terms, and the fact that human beings learn from experience (though not necessarily aright) means that history itself is an influence upon history. The problem of the inducement to invest can therefore probably never be completely settled. But there is hope at least that our ignorance of it can be reduced.

The theory of short-period fluctuations in effective demand, opened up by Mr. Keynes's *General Theory*, has already made great progress. Marx was mainly concerned with long-run dynamic analysis, and this field is still largely untilled. Orthodox academic analysis, bound up with the concept of equilibrium, makes little contribution to it, and the modern theory has not yet gone much beyond the confines of the short period. Changes over the long run in real wages and in the rate of profit, the progress of capital accumulation, the growth and decay of monopoly and the large-scale reactions of changes in technique upon the class structure of society all belong to this field.

Marx, however imperfectly he worked out the details, set himself the task of discovering the law of motion of capitalism, and if there is any hope of progress in economics at all, it must be in using academic methods to solve the problems posed by Marx.

REFERENCES TO "CAPITAL"

(1) Vol. I, chap. 8.   Constant Capital and Variable Capital.

(2) Vol. I, chap. 9.   The Rate of Surplus-Value.   § 1. The Degree of Exploitation of Labour-Power.

(3) Vol. III, chap. 50.   The Semblance of Competition.

(4) Vol. I, chap. 8.   Constant Capital and Variable Capital.

(5) Vol. I, chap. 9.   The Rate of Surplus-Value.   § 1. The Degree of Exploitation of Labour-Power.

(6) Vol. I, chap. 1.   Commodities.   § 1. The Two Factors of a Commodity : Use-Value and Value.

(7) Vol. I, chap. 9.   The Rate of Surplus-Value.   § 1. The Degree of Exploitation of Labour-Power.

(8) Vol. I, chap. 25.   The General Law of Capitalist Accumulation.   § 1. The Increased Demand for Labour-Power that Accompanies Accumulation, the Composition of Capital Remaining the Same.

(9) Vol. III, chap. 2.   The Rate of Profit.

(10) Vol. I, chap. 9.   The Rate of Surplus-Value.   § 1. The Degree of Exploitation of Labour-Power.

(11) Vol. II, chap. 8.   Fixed and Circulating Capital.   § 1. Distinctions of Form.

(12) Vol. III, chap. 4.   The Effect of the Turn-over on the Rate of Profit.

(13) Vol. III, chap. 15.   Unravelling the Internal Contradictions of the Law.   § 2. Conflict between the Expansion of Production and the Creation of Values.

(14) Vol. I, chap. 25.   The General Law of Capitalist Accumulation.   § 3. Progressive Production of a Relative Surplus-Population.

(15) Vol. III, chap. 8.   Different Composition of Capitals in Different Lines of Production and Resulting Differences in the Rates of Profit.

(16) Vol. III, chap. 10.   Compensation of the Average Rate of Profit by Competition.

(17) Vol. III, chap. 12.   Some After Remarks.   § 3. Fluctuations for which the Capitalist makes Allowance.

(18) Vol. III, chap. 10.   Compensation of the Average Rate of
     Profit by Competition.
(19) *Ibid.*
(20) *Ibid.*
(21) Vol. III, chap. 38.   Differential Rent.
(22) Vol. III, chap. 39.   The First Form of Differential Rent.
(23) *Ibid.*
(24) *Ibid.*
(25) Vol. III, chap. 46.   The Price of Land.
(26) Vol. III, chap. 45.   Absolute Ground-Rent.
(27) Vol. I, chap. 1.   Commodities.   § 1. The Two Factors of a
     Commodity : Use-Value and Value.
(28) Vol. I, chap. 7.   The Labour Process and the Process of Pro-
     ducing Surplus-Value.   § 2. The Production of Surplus-
     Value.
(29) Vol. I, chap. 8.   Constant Capital and Variable Capital.
(30) *Ibid.*
(31) *Ibid.*
(32) *Ibid.*
(33) Vol. I, chap. 3.   Money, or the Circulation of Commodities.
     § 1. The Measure of Values.
(34) Vol. I, chap. 5.   Contradictions in the General Formula of
     Capital.
(35) Vol. I, chap. 1.   Commodities.   § 1. The Two Factors of a
     Commodity : Use-Value and Value.
(36) Vol. I, chap. 3.   Money, or the Circulation of Commodities.
     § 2. The Medium of Circulation.
(37) Vol. III, Part VI.   The Transformation of Surplus-Profit into
     Ground-Rent : chap. 37.   Preliminaries.
(38) Vol. I, chap. 1.   Commodities.   § 1. The Two Factors of a
     Commodity : Use-Value and Value.
(39) Vol. I, chap. 11.   Rate and Mass of Surplus-Value.
(40) Vol. III, chap. 9.   Formation of a General Rate of Profit and
     Transformation into Prices of Production.
(41) Vol. III, chap. 45.   Absolute Ground-Rent.
(42) Vol. I, chap. 7.   The Labour Process and the Process of
     Producing Surplus-Value.   § 2. The Production of Surplus
     Value.
(43) Vol. III, chap. 47.   Genesis of Capitalist Ground-Rent.
     § 1. Introductory Remarks.

(44) Vol. I, chap. 8.   Constant Capital and Variable Capital.

(45) Vol. III, chap. 48.   The Trinitarian Formula, § 3.

(46) Vol. I, chap. 12.   The Concept of Relative Surplus-Value.

(47) Vol. I, chap. 25.   The General Laws of Capitalist Accumulation.   § 2. Relative Diminution of the Variable Part of Capital.

(48) Vol. I, chap. 15.   Machinery and Modern Industry.   § 6. The Theory of Compensation as regards the Workpeople displaced by Machinery.

(49) Vol. III, chap. 32.   Money-Capital and Actual Capital (*concluded*).

(50) Vol. I, chap. 32.   Historical Tendency of Capitalist Accumulation.

(51) Vol. III, chap. 17.   Commercial Profit.

(52) Vol. I, chap. 18.   Various Formulæ for the Rate of Surplus-Value.

(53) Vol. III, chap. 10.   Compensation of the Average Rate of Profit by Competition.

(54) Vol. III, chap. 39.   The First Form of Differential Rent.

(55) Vol. II, Part III.   The Reproduction and Circulation of the Aggregate Social Capital : chap. 18.   Introduction.   § 2. The Role of Money Capital.

(56) Vol. III, chap. 49.   A Contribution to the Analysis of the Process of Production.

(57) Vol. I, chap. 1.   Commodities.   § 4. The Fetishism of Commodities and the Secret thereof.

(58) Vol. III, chap. 15.   Unravelling the Internal Contradictions of the Law.   § 4. Supplementary Remarks.

(59) Vol. II, chap. 16.   The Turn-over of the Variable Capital. § 3. The Turn-over of the Variable Capital, considered from the Point of View of Society.

(60) Vol. I, chap. 24.   The Conversion of Surplus-Value into Capital.   § 3. Separation of Surplus-Value into Capital and Revenue.

(61) Vol. III, chap. 15.   Unravelling the Internal Contradictions of the Law.   § 1. General Remarks.

(62) Vol. I, chap. 25.   The General Law of Capitalist Accumulation. § 1. The Increased Demand for Labour-Power that Accompanies Accumulation, the Composition of Capital Remaining the Same.

(63) Vol. I, chap. 25. The General Law of Capitalist Accumulation. § 3. Progressive Production of a Relative Surplus-Population.

(64) *Ibid.*

(65) Vol. I, chap. 6. Buying and Selling of Labour-Power.

(66) Vol. I, chap. 10. The Working Day. § 1. The Limits of the Working Day.

(67) Vol. I, chap. 15. Machinery and Modern Industry. § 3. The Proximate Effects of Machinery on the Workman, (c) Intensification of Labour.

(68) *Ibid.* (a) Appropriation of Supplementary Labour-Power by Capital.

(69) Vol. I, chap. 10. The Working Day. § 5. The Struggle for a Normal Working Day.

(70) Vol. I, chap. 25. The General Law of Capitalist Accumulation. § 1. The Increased Demand for Labour that Accompanies Accumulation, the Composition of Capital Remaining the Same.

(71) *Ibid.* § 3. Progressive Production of a Relative Surplus-Population.

(72) *Ibid.*

(73) *Ibid.*

(74) *Ibid.* § 1. The Increased Demand for Labour-Power that Accompanies Accumulation, the Composition of Capital Remaining the Same.

(75) *Ibid.* § 3. The Progressive Production of a Relative Surplus-Population.

(76) Vol. I, chap. 15. Machinery and Modern Industry. § 9. The Factory Acts.

(77) Vol. I, chap. 14. Division of Labour and Manufacture. § 5. The Capitalist Character of Manufacture.

(78) Vol. I, chap. 17. Changes of Magnitude in the Price of Labour-Power and in Surplus-Value. § 1. Length of the Working Day and Intensity of Labour Constant. Productiveness of Labour Variable.

(79) Vol. III, chap. 14. Counteracting Causes. § 3. Cheapening of the Elements of Constant Capital.

(80) Vol. III, chap. 13. The Theory of the Law.

(81) Vol. III, chap. 14. Counteracting Causes.

(82) *Ibid.* § 1. Raising the Intensity of Exploitation.

(83) *Ibid.* § 2. Depression of Wages below their Value.

(84) Vol. III, chap. 14. Counteracting Causes. § 4. Relative Over-population.

(85) Vol. III, chap. 15. Unravelling the Internal Contradictions of the Law. § 2. Conflict between the Expansion of Production and the Creation of Values.

(86) *Ibid.* § 3. Surplus of Capital and Surplus of Population.

(87) Vol. I, chap. 3. Money, or the Circulation of Commodities. § 2. The Medium of Circulation.

(88) Vol. II, chap. 20. Simple Reproduction. § 2. The Two Departments of Social Production.

(89) *Ibid.* § 1. The Formulation of the Question.

(90) *Ibid.* § 3. The Transactions between the Two Departments.

(91) Vol. II, chap. 20. § 4. Transactions within Department II.

(92) *Ibid.* § 11. Reproduction of the Fixed Capital.

(93) *Ibid.*

(94) Vol. II, chap. 9. The Total Turn-over of Advanced Capital. § 4.

(95) Vol. II, chap. 16. The Turn-over of the Variable Capital. § 3. The Turn-over of the Variable Capital, considered from the Point of View of Society.

(96) *Ibid.*

(97) *Ibid.*

(98) Vol. II, chap. 20. § 11. Reproduction of the Fixed Capital.

(99) *Ibid.* § 12. The Reproduction of the Money Supply.

(100) Vol. II, chap. 21. Accumulation and Reproduction on an Enlarged Scale. § 1. Accumulation in Department I.

(101) Vol. II, chap. 20. Simple Reproduction. § 4. Transactions within Department II.

(102) Vol. II, chap. 16. The Turn-over of the Variable Capital. § 3. The Turn-over of the Variable Capital, considered from the Point of View of Society.

(103) Vol. III, chap. 15. Unravelling the Internal Contradictions of the Law. § 1. General Remarks.

(104) Vol. III, chap. 30. Money-Capital and Actual Capital.

(105) Vol. I, chap. 3. Money, or the Circulation of Commodities. § 2. The Medium of Circulation, (*b*) The Currency of Money.

(106) *Ibid.* § 3. Money, (*b*) Means of Payment.

(107) Vol. III, chap. 22. Rate of Interest.

(108) Vol. III, chap. 15. Unravelling the Internal Contradictions of the Law. § 2. Conflict between the Expansion of Production and the Creation of Values.

(109) Vol. II, chap. 17.   The Circulation of Surplus-Value.   § 1. Simple Reproduction.

(110) Vol. I, chap. 25.   The General Law of Capitalist Accumulation.   § 3. Progressive Production of a Relative Surplus-Population.

(111) Vol. II, chap. 17.   The Circulation of Surplus-Value.   § 1. Simple Reproduction.

(112) *Ibid.*

(113) *Ibid.*

(114) Vol. III, chap. 15.   Unravelling the Internal Contradiction of the Law.   § 2. Conflict between the Expansion of Production and the Creation of Values.

INDEX